PUREN

僕人

Becoming a Great Leader by Becoming a Servant

BY

BROTHER TIMOTHY & RUTH

WORD & SPIRIT
PUBLISHING

Puren
Copyright © 2021 by Brother Timothy & Ruth
ISBN: 978-1-949106-69-5

Published by Word and Spirit Publishing
P.O. Box 701403
Tulsa, Oklahoma 74170
wordandspiritpublishing.com

ACKNOWLEDGEMENTS

People are God's priority and are therefore important to us. Although we have not written down your full names (due to security concerns), you know who you are and what you mean to us and the writing of this book. We love you!

We want to recognize our parents for the loving time and effort spent during our formative years to help us succeed in life. We also want to thank our personal friends who consistently encourage us in so many happy ways . . . mostly by just being there for us!

To our godly advisors and mentors who understood, wisely and correctly, our "process of becoming"—thank you for choosing the "what" and the "timing" of each intervention! Also, our sincere thanks to the hard work and sacrifice of the great pastors and church families who have cared for us (body, soul, and spirit) over the years. Your efforts are still truly appreciated!

Special acknowledgement to the entrepreneurs and business contributors for their financial support which made this book project possible! We pray that the investment you "sowed in love" will produce "fruit" for many generations to come.

Our most sincere thanks to Max—over a short period of time, you have become a personal friend! We are very grateful for you listening to our heart. As we shared our life journey, you translated our story into positive and encouraging words. Thank you for helping to communicate our vision for legacy!

Finally, we want to thank Gasten, Sarah, Bruce, and Mark for their commitment and hard work in getting our story down on paper! You were the "muscle" pushing our pencil!

"But he who is greatest among you shall be your servant."

—MATTHEW 23:11

The Chinese word *Puren* 僕人 is translated *servant*. The idea of being a *Puren* means to become more like Christ, who was the ultimate servant leader.

CONTENTS

PREFACE

In that moment—as I was sitting handcuffed on the floor while they were shouting at me, humiliating me, and harassing me—the scene of Christ's betrayal in the garden of Gethsemane played over and over in my mind. I visualized the moment when Jesus was betrayed by Judas and the way Jesus walked with such love and humility. He was quiet, and I knew I needed to imitate Him.

The police roughly hauled me to the detention center as if I were a POW, all the while trying to terrorize and intimidate me. Once at the cold, concrete compound, they used food and sleep deprivation tactics to wear me down. After they physically and mentally drained my energy reserves, a bright spotlight pierced my eyes as one officer after another shouted at me and grilled me with questions. Their relentless interrogation was intended to exhaust me to the point of collapse. But God is faithful, and He gave me strength in my thoughts as the scene from *The Passion of the Christ* kept replaying in my mind.

They stripped me down to nothing but a T-shirt and underwear. They had two guards on me and they watched me even when I went to the bathroom. I couldn't even do that alone. I remembered in the movie when Jesus prayed to His Father. As I sat in my cold cell, my every move being watched, that scene came to my mind. I asked them if I could just get down on my knees and pray. The guards knew I was a Christian and for some reason they said I could pray. When I prayed, God comforted my heart. I knew if Jesus went through imprisonment for me, God would give me the strength to withstand imprisonment for Him. Jesus was the ultimate *Puren*, and that's what He called me to be.

1

A PARADIGM SHIFT

"For even the Son of Man came not to be served but to serve others and to give his life as a ransom for many."

—Matthew 20:28 NLT

My arms began to ache as the searing Estonian sun beat down upon me. Known for its extreme Baltic cold, on this summer day the weather was anything but. The three bags stuffed with empty glass bottles that I was holding felt more like bricks and were getting heavier with each breath. Exhausted and frustrated, I let out a deep sigh. Not only were my arms hurting, my feet were throbbing. How long had I been standing in this line? Could it possibly move any slower? This was worse than going through security check in the airport! *"Why am I even here, God?"* I grumbled while shifting my bodyweight from one leg to the other. *"This is not what I came here for."*

Just a few days earlier I had been relaxing in my comfortable four-bedroom home back in the United States. The year was 1986 and though I was a successful engineer, God had put a heavy call on my life for missions. As a fourth generation convert of Hudson Taylor, his legacy had been passed down to me and like him, I was passionate about reaching the lost. I also understood that one of the key principles for success in life was the ability to create and execute a skillful plan with precision. That philosophy had served me well as an engineer, and that was how I approached my calling to evangelism. If God said it, then that was the way it would be. Well, God had said it. He wanted to have a great move in the Soviet Union, and as a zealous Chinese American Christian, I believed I was the man for the job. My plan was all set and I was eager to execute it!

Several years before this experience, my wife Ruth and I had been introduced to a wonderful Christian brother from Estonia named Pastor Rei. I just knew that if we were to travel to Estonia and work with him, God would use us to spark a great Estonian Revival. Pastor Rei graciously opened the door for us to come. With excitement, Ruth and I announced to our family and friends that we would be traveling to Estonia to bring about a great move of God. I envisioned myself before crowds of Estonians and Russians, preaching with such a powerful anointing that everyone who heard me would be moved to repentance and would cry out to God for salvation. I was God's man for the hour, and with this confidence, I was more than willing to foot the bill for the airfare and hotel.

After paying $2,500 (at the time a large sum of money) for our basic economy flight tickets, we had to pay $150 each night (this was a lot of money as well) for our "no frills" communist-style accommodations. Estonia was under Soviet rule during this time and the majority of the buildings were dismal and depressing shades of brown and gray. Yet, Ruth and I felt encouraged that our financial sacrifice would reap big rewards in the harvest of souls that was about to take place. Our sense of God's purpose for this trip was strong. Without a doubt, we were on the brink of a great move of God!

Once we arrived, I was enthusiastic to get to work and see *my* plan implemented! There was no time to waste. Because we had been preparing for the trip for quite a while, I assumed Pastor Rei had all my speaking engagements lined up as well as some kind of larger evangelistic gathering.

As Pastor Rei and his wife warmly greeted us, I constrained my zeal and responded with a cool, calm smile of my own. *We are here now with a message from God for your people,* I thought to myself while giving the pastor a reassuring pat on the shoulder. *Everything will be okay, brother.* That is what I thought. What came out of my mouth however, was, "We are so happy to serve you in any way that we can!"

But did I even understand those words? I thought so. After all, we had sacrificed much to get there and wanted to make the most of our two weeks. The people were starving spiritually and time was of the essence.

"Where will my first speaking engagements be?" I asked the pastor as smoothly as I could. "Which churches will we be ministering to throughout the weekend?"

"My brother," Pastor Rei replied, "we don't have any meetings lined up for you, but I would enjoy you visiting with my wife and me in our home."

To say I was shocked and disappointed would be an understatement. Yet, wanting to be a "good" Christian I answered, "That's okay, brother. Praise the Lord!" Inside, my heart was sinking. Here I had already spent $2,500 on the airfare and was paying $150 a night for a bare-bones hotel room. Was it all for nothing? Little did I know that a great move of God was about to take place, just not like I expected. The Holy Spirit had to take me all the way to Estonia, not to change them, but to change me. The biggest work of God in Estonia was in *my own heart*. My vision and perspective would be ripped to shreds, replaced by something much more powerful that would prepare me for a lifetime of missions instead of a two-week stint.

The weekend arrived and Pastor Rei and his wife invited us to their home for breakfast. When we arrived, the pastor was standing in his kitchen wearing his wife's apron, ready to prepare our meal. Later, as we were visiting, Pastor Rei's wife called him into the kitchen where she was working. They began speaking in Estonian and I had no idea what they were discussing. Soon, he came back into the living area carrying heavy bags of glass bottles that needed to be returned to the recycling center. Under the former Soviet regime, the people returned bottles and other recyclables to recoup some of their money. Pastor Rei and I gathered up more bags filled with empty bottles, and with great difficulty, crammed them and ourselves into his Russian mini-car.

Once we arrived at the recycling center, I carefully helped Pastor Rei unload the heavy bags. We each had to carry three. The courtyard of the center was crowded with others doing the exact same thing. I had no idea what the process was like because in the States we did not use this system. Being a "good Christian," I smiled and told Pastor Rei that I was glad to help, even as I concealed my growing frustration and fatigue.

Standing there in the hot, summer sun, I noticed a shopping cart sitting idly off to one side. Being the "smart" one, I decided to put the cart to use. As I placed the last of my bags into the cart however, I was suddenly slapped with a verbal assault consisting entirely of angry Russian words. A little Russian woman with a triangular scarf wrapped around her head marched towards me yelling and vehemently gesturing with her hands. I did not understand Russian, nor did I understand the culture, but I clearly understood her anger. Completely oblivious to the apparent crime that I had just committed, I quickly gathered up all the bags and returned her cart. That seemed to calm the woman a bit, yet I was growing more and more agitated. Here I was, "God's man of the hour," stuck holding bags of glass bottles in the hot sun. My arms were not accustomed to this type of work and I was ready to leave. But again, I wanted to be a "good Christian" so I said nothing.

Finally, after way too long, we made it to the front of the line. I was so relieved and thought we could finally return to the house. To my disappointment however, I noticed that now we had to count each bottle for the cashier and then carefully place them one-by-one into the correct slot of the correct crate. The slots had to match the bottle size. I could not believe it! But once again I said *nothing*, though I was fuming on the inside.

Pastor Rei, who had been doing this process for thirty years, quickly placed all the bottles from his bag into the proper crates. He knew instinctively which size bottle would fit in which slot and was done in five minutes. I, on the other hand, was completely unfamiliar with the process and finally emerged thirty minutes later. It was then that I realized—to my great dismay—that I needed to stand in yet another line.

This one was to give my ticket to the attendant who would calculate how much money I was to receive for the bottle returns. Impatiently standing in that line, I could not help thinking, *When I left the USA, I told everyone that I was going to be used by God to change Estonia, and now here I am doing nothing! And I spent so much money just to be here.*

By this time, Pastor Rei and I had been at the center for almost two hours. I was hot, dehydrated, and ready to be done. My only solace was that surely my pastor friend would be recouping a significant amount of money for our combined efforts. After I handed the attendant my ticket, she began to calculate on her old, dilapidated machine the amount of money that was owed in exchange for the bottles. She began to count, "One, two, three, four, five, six," and she stopped. There in my sweaty palm rested six rubles, the equivalent of one US dollar. I was stunned. We had spent all that time and gone through all that trouble, for a *dollar! If you needed a dollar,* my mind raced, *you could have just asked me rather than having us go through all this trouble! I would have given you a dollar! Or ten dollars or even a hundred to avoid having to go through this nonsense!*

Then, while staring down at the six rubles resting in my palm, something completely unexpected, humbling, and *supernatural* happened. God gave me a vision of Jesus hanging on the cross peering down at me. In my mind, it was as if I were standing at His feet right there at Calvary. As His eyes pierced me to my core, I had the keen understanding that He had come down from heaven into our world, not only to die, but to live among us, particularly as a persecuted Jew. Jesus would have identified easily with Pastor Rei's way of life because He lived among the people as one of them, serving them, for thirty years before He began His official ministry. Suddenly, it came to me that I had no way of identifying with these people because I wasn't focused on them but rather on doing some great spiritual work. Though I came to Estonia to serve God and the people, this trip was really about *me* and *my personal agenda.*

My heart felt such pain as I imagined Jesus going through the struggles that He must have faced during the process of daily living. I had never before identified with that particular type of pain that Christ must have felt—the King of the universe humbling Himself and living as a peasant. Right there in the middle of the courtyard, tears began streaming down my cheeks. If Jesus had used my mentality, He would have come down from heaven for a short-term mission trip where He would have stayed in a nice place, maybe taught a few sermons, and then died on the cross to redeem all of mankind. But He didn't.

Jesus came as a baby in a manger, not as an adult. For thirty years He lived as a son learning obedience. As a

Jewish carpenter, He too struggled to make a living under Roman occupation. In essence, Jesus delivered bottles for years before, at the age of thirty, He began the mission His Father ultimately had called Him to. Then, Jesus spent three years with His disciples—teaching them, walking with them, washing their feet, and living life with them. After thirty-three years, knowing what it was like to be fully human, Jesus died on the cross to pay for our sins.

This was an epiphany moment for me. God's way of doing missions was completely contrary to my Western missionary mindset. I had traveled to Estonia with the idea that I was "God's man of the hour," ready to preach and change their world in two weeks and then return home the victor. Yet, through this divine encounter with Jesus during my first weekend in Estonia, God transformed my way of thinking. I realized that I did not understand God's heart for missions or the Estonian people—how they lived and struggled with daily living. As I continued to feel the eyes of Jesus piercing me, I wept because, in that moment, it became crystal clear to me that I did not possess the heart of a servant. I had no idea how to love people to the degree that Jesus loved them, but I would learn.

A Servant's Heart

The Holy Spirit impressed upon my spirit that before I could truly serve, I first needed to learn how to have the *heart* of a servant. I had arrived in Estonia to do *my* great "work" without having God's heart or knowing His will. In my Western mindset, I just wanted to show up, do my work (have people move out of my way so that I could build what I came to build), and then return home. With my mouth I had continuously declared that I had come to serve, but in reality, I had no idea what *serving* and *having a servant's heart* actually meant. While delivering the bottles, I was thinking, *"Why did I pay $2,500 for the airfare and $150 a night for the hotel and come all this way for this? Where was my platform?"* Yet, through this experience, God reshaped my entire worldview on missions for the rest of my life. As the tears streamed down my face, I realized what a *servant's heart* really meant. As I was crying, I heard the voice of Pastor Rei, "Brother, are you all right?" He was watching me weeping, but didn't see me interacting with anyone.

"I'm okay," I said, wiping the tears from my eyes. "I just had an encounter with God."

My spiritual eyes had been opened to the true reason the Holy Spirit had brought me to this exact place to deliver bottles.

Becoming Like Christ

In Estonia, God changed me from wanting to accomplish something for Him, to wanting to give my life, asking nothing in return. When we serve God, we must seek to be like Him instead of serving for Him by pushing our personal agenda of what we think needs to be accomplished. God does not expect me to *do* anything, nor does He want anything from me, if I do not first desire to be like Him. It's possible to serve without giving our lives, but God wants us to serve *by* giving our lives and becoming like Christ. Once we desire to be like Him, our works and actions will please Him, because our hearts are His.

Often, people try to do things *for* God, without actually doing the things *of* God. God wants our lives before He wants our service. He doesn't want our performance. He wants a relationship. It's out of intimacy with Him in a genuine relationship that we begin to be transformed into His image, which is having the heart of a servant. Before my experience in Estonia, I was ready to *do* missions my way, coming with my own head knowledge, power, resources, degrees, and human accolades. Yet, my plan and pattern for missions was not God's plan and pattern. God desired that I become like a servant, submitting to His authority, Pastor Rei's authority, and the local leaders. My experience of carrying the bottles was purposed by God to change and *revolutionize* me in serving Him. It wasn't just so that I could do a good deed. God wanted to alter my heart so that I could become more like Christ. Through that experience, God shifted my paradigm. *I had come to Estonia as a teacher, but I was leaving as a learner who was submitted to God's plan and pattern.* God does not want our good works, our head knowledge, or our resources. He wants our lives. Are you willing to give yours?

Questions for Reflection

1. Have you thought about the difference between doing things *for* God versus doing the things *of* God?

2. Do you serve God with His agenda or with yours?

3. Are you serving with the mentality of a "teacher" (having nothing to learn) or with the humility of a *learner* (learning while serving)?

2

THE AMERICAN DREAM
VS. GOD'S DREAM

*"Paul, a bondservant of Jesus Christ, called to be an apostle,
separated to the gospel of God. . ."*

—Romans 1:1

Many years ago, when I was a young executive rising in business, I believed I was a servant of Christ. I went to church, took part in different ministries, and thought I truly loved God. During that time, Ruth and I were considered "DINKs." This stands for "Double Income, No Kids." People in this category usually have plenty of extra money and few time-constraints beyond their jobs. We were caught up in the "DINK" lifestyle and both of us were highly successful. Paying cash for trips abroad and other such activities was no problem. Climbing the corporate ladder, I was seeking success. Of course, we were Christians and regularly attended a church where I was considered a leader—a servant of Christ. *Yep, that was me . . .* or so I thought.

As a Chinese American who had risen to prominence in the corporate world, I had prestige and use of the corporate jet. This allowed me to travel anywhere in the United States and frequently to China to broker deals. Some of the deals could have potentially brought in billions of dollars for my company, which only fueled my pride and self-assurance. Surely, I had it all!

Then one evening, something happened to me while I was watching the television show, *Lifestyles of the Rich and Famous.* Some of you may remember it. It was one of the first shows to feature the homes and lives of the super-wealthy. Fascinated by the way the rich and famous lived, the things of this world still tugged on my heart. I loved seeing the ornate gardens, lavish yachts, private jets, and exotic cars. During a commercial break, while flipping the channels I just happened upon an interview with the American evangelist, Arthur Blessitt, who had walked across the China country-side carrying a twelve-foot wooden cross.

As he was relating the story, he said the Chinese people came out of their villages and lined both sides of the streets to watch this 6'2" American lug a big wooden stick down the road. Most had no idea what it meant. They thought he must have been an international sports promoter doing some sort of marathon or something. The symbolism of the cross never registered in their mind. They had no idea that the cross represented salvation! And they didn't know that Jesus had died on the cross for their sins. They had never been told! Then it hit me. Hundreds of thousands of Chinese people have died without ever knowing Jesus! I was heartbroken. What made me deserve to know Christ when all these people didn't?

Here I was in my comfortable home, with a wonderful job, watching *Lifestyles of the Rich and Famous* while my own people were perishing. A floodgate unleashed inside of me as the Holy Spirit tugged on my heart. I got down on my knees and put my hands on the television and cried out to God. *I wept.* I wept for China. I wept for the people who were lost and dying without Christ. Millions of people in China were in darkness while I was resting in the light. Dropping to my knees, I cried, "Oh God! What am I doing here in the USA? Please send me to my people!" Afterwards, though nothing had changed on the outside, God had heard my prayer and began setting things in motion towards the call He had placed upon my life.

Once we surrender to God and embrace His purposes for us, the Holy Spirit can then get to work. God is looking for people with hearts surrendered to Him. It may not happen overnight, but as you begin to allow your heart to be broken by the things that break God's heart, He will begin to move the chess pieces around in your life. God will arrange things so that you continue to walk toward the call He has placed on you. There was still work to be done in my heart, but the seeds were planted. The Holy Spirit was moving me toward the place of becoming God's *servant*.

Though God was working on me under the surface, I was the same business-minded guy, obsessed with climbing the corporate ladder. And as a Chinese American, there was always a level of competition between me and some of my Chinese American colleagues. My company had a highly coveted position working as a corporate interpreter to the other Chinese businesses we were working with. When they were in the process of recruiting for this position, more than 100 Chinese Americans submitted applications. It was fiercely competitive and my pride continued to grow when I made it to the top twenty . . . then the top ten . . . then the top five!

The person chosen would work with the CEO and the top executives to broker some of the biggest deals for our organization. Eventually, it was down to the top two—one other person that I worked with and me! My company was looking for someone with PR ability, technical expertise, a command of the Chinese language, and advanced oral skills that could connect with the businessmen from China. When they finally chose me, I felt like I had reached the pinnacle of my career!

I would regularly fly to different parts of the United States and China with the CEO and key company executives. We would stay in five-star accommodations as we met with the businessmen from China, and whenever they came to visit, I would host them. I would simply call for the corporate jet and take them anywhere in the United States they wanted to go. For example, I could take them to Disney World or fly them to New York City, and charge everything to an unlimited budget account. Those things are not wrong in themselves. But I was so proud! While I was a Christian, I was not a servant of Christ. I was a servant to success. Climbing the corporate ladder, money, and fame were my true gods.

Tiananmen Square

But things change when God captivates our hearts. Things happen. We change. Our perspective changes. We begin to see through God's eyes. During one of my trips to China, I had landed in Beijing and was staying in a five-star hotel near Tiananmen Square. Late in the afternoon, I decided to take a stroll through the square. As I walked, people were every-where—thousands of them, swirling all around me. Pride also welled up inside me as a Chinese American. Here I was in a five-star hotel while most of these Chinese people were still making a few dollars a day. Right then, while pondering how I had arrived, the Holy Spirit quickened to my heart. *"Son, look around at all these people. Is there any difference between you and them?"*

I looked around and answered, "No. They are Chinese. They have dark hair like me. They have eyes like me. They eat food with chopsticks like me. I don't see any difference." Continuing to walk, the time passed and I wondered why God had asked me this question.

"Look again," the Holy Spirit said. *"Is there any difference between you and them?"*

By now, the sun was beginning to set, and as I gazed back over the throng, their features were more like shadowy silhouettes. I knew they all still looked like me. I was Chinese. They were Chinese. But this time they were hidden because of the darkness. Watching the shadows moving about, I realized that there was a light shining on me. Then, it dawned on me that while I was one of the 1.3 billion Chinese in the world, for some reason, God had brought me into the light and not these others. "Why, God," I asked, "Why was I **not** born in China like all these people? Why were my family members the ones who became Christians through Hudson Taylor? I could have been a communist! An atheist! A Buddhist! Why am I a fourth generation Christian?"

I began to realize that I was incredibly fortunate to be born in the free world and to be able to come to America. Other people my age that were born in China were greatly affected by the Cultural Revolution; people of my generation who were born in China were the ones who were bringing upheaval. Lawless young students, they were known as the Red Guards. They wreaked havoc in the nation, even persecuting their own parents. But the revolution backfired and today, many of them have menial jobs like washing public bathroom toilets, sweeping streets, etc. They live in a dark pit of hopelessness and it could have just as easily been me. The Cultural Revolution could have ruined me. "Why did You save me, God? Why was I fortunate enough to receive such a high-level college education?" God had blessed me with an excellent job. He had given me an amazing wife and a great home in a comfortable environment with many material blessings. "Why, God, did You let me have all these things? Why did You choose to save me? Why am I so special from others?" My shoulders slumped as I stood there and wept! It seemed weeping was becoming a regular occurrence for me as the Holy Spirit dealt with me more and more.

"*I AM that I AM,*" God interrupted. He was communicating to me His supremacy and sovereignty. "*I AM your God. I AM your provider.*" In other words, He was nicely saying to me, "Shut up. It is not for you to question why. It's for you to tell Me, 'I'm willing to obey.' You may not understand the things I do, but it is important what you do with what I've given you. *'For everyone to whom much is given, from him much will be required; and to whom much has been committed, of him they will ask the more'"* (Luke 12:48). That's when I began to see there was a purpose for my life much bigger than making money and climbing the ladder of success.

When I was a young man, God gave me a vision in a dream. I was standing on a bridge suspended in timeless space. On one side of the bridge, I saw the word "West," and on the other side of the bridge, I could see the word "East." As I pondered this, the Lord spoke to my heart that He was going to use my life to bridge the East with the West. Like Jesus had invited Peter to drop his nets and become a fisher of men, God was calling me to be a fisher of the Chinese people. My life would be a bridge, leading many to Jesus. But would I obey?

I cried out that night in Tiananmen Square saying, "God, I want to live for You! I want to live Your way, not my way!" This is the voice of a servant driven by *love*. Slowly but surely, God was opening my eyes to see what it meant to have the heart of a servant. Up to that point, my life had been all about me. Even as a child in Asia, I had dreamt about going to the United States one day to seek freedom and financial prosperity. Highly motivated and driven, I studied extra hard to get the high scores needed to receive a scholarship for advanced education. After reaching that goal, my entire purpose had been to land a high paying, secure job. That would be the ultimate—making a lot of money to satisfy my own desires and dreams. Now, I had worked tirelessly to climb the corporate ladder where I could be connected with the CEOs and top executives. But my experience with God in Tiananmen Square had wrecked *my* plans and showed me that there was much more to life than the things I was living for. Sure, I had worked hard, but it was God, by His grace, who had placed me in the environment where I could be blessed with opportunity. This was a new revelation for me.

If God had not graciously moved my family out of China, I would not have had any of the things I was currently enjoying. There was a shift in my perspective that night. I began to see and feel God's heart for all the Chinese people that were living in darkness. Deep within my core, a burden for lost souls was welling up. God was changing me. However, God's overhaul of my heart was only beginning.

Becoming a Bondservant

When God began to work on my heart, He began to move things around in my life so I would no longer be a *slave* to these other things. He was about to make me His *bondservant*. A bondservant is someone who is motivated by loving his master and is willing to work or do service without wages or recognition. As I was basking in my career success, the company I worked for began to go through some corporate transitions which included downsizing. They systematically went through the organization and more than 900 people were laid off!

Yet, because I had worked together with the company CEO, and had seen such success, I wasn't too worried. In fact, I was feeling pretty confident. But I remember the day I walked into the office and the atmosphere had changed—the air was tense. Nobody was talking or looking at each other. My boss asked me to meet him in the conference room. When we walked in, there was a woman I had never seen sitting quietly off to the side. I didn't say anything to her. Once seated, my boss read to me the script for laying people off. As he did, pride and anger erupted inside me. *"How dare you lay me off! Don't you know who I am? Don't you know I travel with the CEO?"*

"Who is this lady?" I asked. "And why is she here while you're telling me this? What is she sitting here for?" My boss was actually trembling! He knew that I worked closely with the CEO and he was nervous about giving me the news.

"This lady was sent from the Stress Center," he replied. "She is a psychologist, and she is here just in case you don't take the news well."

In that moment, I realized how far away my heart had drifted. Now, here I sat, at the mercy of a humanistic psychologist to save my soul. *Oh, how far I had fallen.* I was going to church and doing all the right things, yet my heart was not surrendered to God. Colossians 1:18 says, *"And He is the head of the body, the church, who is the beginning, the firstborn from the dead, that in all things He may have the preeminence."* But I wasn't really concerned with His purposes, at least not enough to let them change my life. I was shocked at the state of my soul and how pride was ruling me. Looking at my boss, I simply responded, "Okay," signed the pink slip, and walked out the door.

The company was gracious and provided us with a grace period that let us continue working for two months while searching for new employment. Most companies handed you a layoff notice and that was it. Two months was a long time and much appreciated. Still, each day was a struggle as I wrestled with my pride. I had gone from being a *superstar* to being a *falling star.* Though I'd been hand-picked over hundreds of Chinese Americans for this prestigious position, it meant nothing because now I would be standing in the unemployment line like everybody else that was laid off.

Amazingly, when I went home to tell Ruth the bad news she wasn't shaken in the least. "Praise the Lord," she responded with compassion and understanding. "God has other plans for your life." Little did I know that for months she had been praying for me. Ruth prayed I would not be caught up with seeking after money or trying to live the lifestyle of the rich and famous. She was also praying her husband would love God more than he loved the things of the world. (There is a lot to say about the power of a wife's prayers.) Ruth knew my heart was seeking after the wrong things, and she knew my heart wasn't following the call and purpose God had for me. Even now, looking back, I'm amazed at how loving she always was to me as I was sliding toward my pursuit of worldly success. Ruth prayed with fervency that God would get hold of me. I am so thankful for her loving, powerful prayers!

God answered her prayers in a dynamic way. One night, after crying out to Him because of my situation, He met me while I was sleeping. In a dream, I was looking at the calendar on February 1, thinking how this would be my first day out of work. I would be standing in an unemployment line, waiting to get a check. Frantic, I woke up in a cold sweat, the hairs on the back of my neck standing up! The thought of waiting in the unemployment line was overwhelming. Rolling out of bed, I fell flat on my face before God. My heart was pounding so loud, I thought it might wake Ruth. "God," I silently pleaded, "I can't take this anymore! Rescue me!" I was at the end of myself. I had worked and done so many things in my own strength, but God had brought me to a place of realizing that I could not do anything without Him. Laying on the floor, the Holy Spirit whispered, "*Stretch out your hands.*" So, I stretched my hands out before Him in obedience. Then, in my spirit, I saw the Lord put handcuffs on me. He said, "*Son, today, you are no longer working with your own hands. I have put spiritual handcuffs on you. From this day forward, I will lead you on My path. No longer your way, but now My way.*" His voice was so clear. The handcuffs symbolized that I no longer worked with my hands because I was now surrendered to Him completely! I was His servant. Not my will, but His will be done!

When I woke up, the stress and anxiety I had been carrying for so long was gone. The burden lifted. From that day until the final day of my two months in the office, I was able to go to work with a peace and confidence. Everybody who was laid off was busy sending out resumes, but the company specifically stipulated that nobody who had been laid off was allowed to submit one or apply for any other positions within the company. As part of the downsizing policy, you could not go to another department. While everyone else was sending out their resumes, God told me not to. Instead, He told me to just hold steady, wait on Him, and follow His leading. In obedience to that prompting, I did not send out a single resume and worked every day as if I hadn't been laid off. With a joyful heart, I *served* my employer as if I would be working there indefinitely. No longer was I trying to impress my boss. I just wanted to give God glory.

People thought I was out of my mind. They couldn't understand how I could work with such a great attitude in the midst of my current circumstances. But it wasn't me. It was the power of the Holy Spirit inside me. Supernaturally, my heart was at complete rest as I trusted the Lord.

Three days before February 1, I received a phone call from the manager of another department head. He worked closely with the CEO and heard I had been a part of the mass layoff. He wanted to talk with me so I went up to his office. "I don't know what happened to you with these layoffs," he said, "but I wanted to talk to you. As I was recently negotiating my contract about some new business deals we have in China, I told them I want you to be the one to travel with me. You are the best interpreter and negotiator I have traveled with. You know the technology well, but you also know how to deal with people well. If you are willing, I want you to work for me." The first thing that came into my mind was our company's policy that we weren't allowed to take a job for another department. As I was thinking about this, he told me I could get back to him in two or three days, and that I didn't have to worry about the details.

I told my wife what happened and we prayed for the next two days. After praying, we both had peace about this position. I went back and told him I would accept his job offer. I was hired in that new role on January 31, just *one day* before the layoff became effective. Not only did I not lose my job, I also received a thirty percent raise and a promotion! I had surrendered my life to God and God did what I couldn't do on my own. I learned a priceless lesson. I didn't have to work with my own strength. Instead, I could be completely surrendered to God and trust Him with my whole life. He is my Jehovah-Jireh that supplies all my needs.

The Chicken and the Eagle

Through this experience, I learned to be an *eagle, not a chicken!* What does this mean you might be wondering? God taught me that I could not succeed in my own strength or by my own ability. But, like an eagle that has faith in the wind to carry it, I needed to trust the Holy Spirit to carry me to new heights. Now that God had shown me that a bondservant is passionate about God and motivated by love, I realized more than ever that I wanted to soar upon the wisdom and the power of the Lord, letting His strength carry me!

The Lord revealed to me that I had been living as a chicken, not in the sense of being scared, but by being a lowly, everyday, barnyard animal that couldn't fly. I was trying to accomplish a simple yet impossible task—like a chicken trying to jump over a fence. Let me explain. Chickens can barely fly because of their tiny wings. It's almost laughable to think about a chicken soaring while their little wings desperately flap in the air and their fat little bodies drag them back to the ground. A chicken thinks he can accomplish anything. Yet he can only flap and flap and flap! But if we think of an eagle resting on a rock, a completely different image comes into our minds. An eagle will wait until he feels the *current* underneath his wings, then, at the right time, he will stretch out his wings and begin to soar to unimaginable heights with seemingly little effort, letting the wind do the work.

Isaiah 40:31 says, *"But those who wait on the Lord shall renew their strength; they shall mount up with wings like eagles, they shall run and not be weary, they shall walk and not faint."* I was born to be an eagle and yet, all this time, like a chicken I was desperately flapping my tiny wings, trying to jump over a little fence in my own strength. But God was telling me I was born an eagle, that all I had to do was wait on Him—wait for His strength. God was calling me to be like the eagle and wait up on the high cliff until the wind of the Holy Spirit came and then simply open up my wings and soar! I was no longer the chicken. Now I was an eagle soaring on the wind by the strength of the Spirit never to be the same!

Are you a chicken or an eagle? Are you desperately flapping your little chicken wings trying to jump over the fences in your life? Or do you want to be like the eagle, waiting for the wind of the Holy Spirit to lift you where you need to go? Our heart's cry needs to be, *"Lord, lift me up. Carry me in Your strength. Let me be the eagle that I was born to be."* Today, choose to wait on the Lord and soar like an eagle on the wind of the Holy Spirit. You too will never be the same.

After the job transition, and until the day God called me into full-time ministry on the mission field, I worked in that department, but no longer with strife and self-strength. Now I was filled with God's Spirit of peace, joy, and rest! I had become an eagle! So, when the day came to go into the mission field, it was easy because God had already done the work inside me. Even though I continued to work for five more years at that company, I was not the same. God had taken my heart and my hands. Instead of being a bondservant of money and success, I had become a bondservant of God.

The Love of a Bondservant

Many times in Western culture, we become so busy trying to be a great leader with influence that we lose sight of our ultimate purpose in Jesus. If Jesus is our greatest example, then we must remember what Jesus did and who He was. Jesus was a *servant*. He served us out of love—even unto His own death. True followers of Christ are servants, but more than that, they are *bondservants*.

When I think about the love of a bondservant, I think of Paul the Apostle. In the book of Acts, we read about the bold, courageous way he pioneered new territory for the gospel. Paul was fearless. He endured shipwrecks, was beaten with rods, stoned, left for dead, and arrested repeatedly. He suffered in prison, endured pain, yet never wavered in his faith or his commitment. Something deep within Paul's core kept him forging forward despite his hardships. Paul had an unquenchable, internal fire. This fire, this passion, this unwavering commitment, is what I refer to as the *love of a bondservant*. A love for His master! Only a love commitment this deep could move Paul to endure through such difficulty.

In Romans 1:1, Paul gives us insight into what motivated him when he identified himself as a bondservant. He had the right to use a variety of titles. After all, Paul had visited the third heaven and would pen most of the New Testament in his lifetime. He could have addressed his readers as, "Paul: international speaker, worldwide church planter, world-renowned author, and multicultural evangelist." You get the idea. But he didn't. Paul called himself something else entirely. This man who turned cities and countries upside down identified himself as a *bondservant*. Paul knew his identity in Christ; and he knew he was a slave of love. Why was Paul so filled with zeal and fiery passion? It was because he was in love with his Savior.

So, what exactly is a bondservant? A bondservant is a *love slave* (someone who chooses to serve another because of their love for that person or cause). A *love slave* doesn't serve for personal glory or gain. In the same way, a bondservant loves his master so much that he is willing to lay down all of his own rights and all of his own desires to serve. This idea of a bondservant comes from the Old Testament. Deuteronomy 15:12-17 gives a detailed explanation of this concept:

"If your brother, a Hebrew man, or a Hebrew woman, is sold to you and serves you six years, then in the seventh year you shall let him go free from you. And when you send him away free from you, you shall not let him go away empty-handed; you shall supply him liberally from your flock, from your threshing floor, and from your winepress. From what the Lord your God has blessed you with, you shall give to him. You shall remember that you were a slave in the land of Egypt, and the Lord your God redeemed you; therefore I command you this thing today. And if it happens that he says to you, 'I will not go away from you,' because he loves you and your house, since he prospers with you, then you shall take an awl and thrust it through his ear to the door, and he shall be your servant forever. Also to your female servant you shall do likewise."

In the Hebrew culture, if another Hebrew was your slave, he was to go free after seven years. And he was not just to go free, but he was to be well-supplied. The slave was to be blessed and sent away with abundance. And this wasn't a token blessing. Deuteronomy instructs the master to give liberally. He was to give him meat, grain, and wine. This gift from the master's house was enough money for the servant to start a new life successfully. This is just like what God did for us. We were slaves, and He set us free!

Not only did Jesus set us free, but also, He blessed us with heavenly blessings. The rest of this passage in Deuteronomy gives us insight into why Paul served with such zeal. It tells us about a different kind of slave. This is not a slave that just wants to go free, take the blessings, and start a new life on their own. No, this is a slave who loves their master so much that they are willing to give up their entire life to serve him as a *slave!*

Love-Slave

A normal slave was released after seven years, but a bondservant was a bondservant (or love-slave) for life. They laid down their lives because of *love*. And they laid down their lives knowing they would never take them back up again. This was a lifelong *love* commitment. When Paul called himself a love-slave, he was saying that his life was completely given to His master—laid down forever because of his deep love. He was a bondservant, a *love-slave!*

As I was meditating on this passage, a picture came to my mind of a slave that had just been released by his master. Not only had he been released, but he was loaded up with blessings, gifts, and treasures for him to begin his new life. As this particular slave began down the road, he suddenly stopped. Looking back over his shoulder that was weighed down with a bundle of wine and oil, he took one last look at his master. When he did, his heart seized. Love overtook him. Dropping his gifts to the ground, the slave raced back and threw himself at the feet of his master.

"Master!" he cried. "I don't want to leave you! Please, I would rather stay and serve you for the rest of my life than to have all these gifts and livestock because being with you—knowing you—is the greatest blessing of all!" At this, the master took the slave to the doorpost and drove the awl through the slave's earlobe. From that moment on, he chose to be a voluntary slave because of the love he had for his master. Being with the master meant more than simply having all his blessings—it meant love!

This is exactly what happened for Ruth and me when we left America and our jobs. When my company rehired me, I received a significant pay raise and was promoted with a great pension. But when God asked us to leave for the mission field, we gave it all up. We made a choice. We wanted Jesus more. We wanted to *be* more like Jesus. We wanted to serve our heavenly Father more. We wanted His plan and purpose for our lives more because we chose to be Christ's *love-slaves*.

While in the United States working at our secular jobs, God taught us what it meant to be bondservants. We knew the time would come when we would be serving God in China; however, before that could happen, God had much more to teach us. This came while serving Him in Estonia. After God had worked so much in our hearts, Ruth and I decided to accept God's call to serve in Estonia as bondservants. We accepted this call, because we loved our Master Jesus even more than we loved the blessings He had given us. We loved His *presence* and His Kingdom more than we loved the security of our paychecks and the comfort of our home and lives in America. We wanted to be love-slaves for Christ. *"To live is Christ, and to die is gain"* (Philippians 1:21).

Accepting God's call is important, whatever that call may be. For us, it was the foreign mission field. For some people, God has called them to accept a job in their community to be a light and an influence. He may call some to a financial or influential position so they can be a resource for missions around the world. God changed our hearts during the time we worked in the professional corporate arena. During that time, we gave generous financial contributions to local and international mission efforts. We gave our time and gifts for that effort, as well as working in our professions. God may not call everyone to leave everything for the mission field, but He called us. And our hearts were ready and willing to obey whenever, whatever, and wherever God's calling took us.

In most cultures today, this concept of being a *bondservant* is not a popular teaching or a regular topic of conversation. You won't hear too many sermon series about how to become more like a slave. But this is a concept we need to understand if we really want God to use our lives for His glory. Paul was able to do extraordinary things because he understood that his life was not his own; he was so in love with Jesus that he chose to become a *bondservant*. Just as Paul was driven by his love for Christ, I found myself on the mission field driven by the same passion and love for Christ, serving Him as a *love-slave*. My greatest joy in life was no longer the blessings that the Master gave to Ruth and me. Now my greatest joy was serving Him wholeheartedly because of my love for Him!

Questions for Reflection

1. In what areas of your life are you soaring like an eagle or flapping your wings like a chicken?

2. What is it like when you hear from the Lord about your calling?

3. Have you struggled to let go of your own dream? What was that experience like for you, and how did you respond?

4. Do you treasure the way God brings changes and brokenness into your life? What have you learned from those experiences?

3

THE UNDER-ROWER

"As each has received a gift, use it to serve one another, as good stewards of God's varied grace."

—1 Peter 4:10 ESV

With muscles flexing and calloused hands gripping the oars, the men below keep their unbroken pace like the perpetual rhythm of a heartbeat. All the while, those up on deck and in the cabins carry on their normal business, as the ship moves briskly through the water, powered by the steady rowing of the slaves beneath the ship. There was no glamour or glory for these slaves forced into a life of relentless rowing on an ancient Roman battleship. There was no view of the beautiful landscape outside, only of the dark and soggy wooden planks, the weathered oar underhand, and the sweaty backs of the slaves laboring in front of them. Hot, humid, breathing in foul and musty air, the work was grueling while those above deck remained oblivious as they took in the fresh ocean breeze blowing across their faces. They were free to go about their affairs while the human-powered engine below propelled the vessel to its assigned destination.

"Let a man so consider us," wrote Paul in 1 Corinthians 4:1, *"as servants of Christ and stewards of the mysteries of God."* In this passage, the term *"servant"* comes from the Greek word *huperetes,* which means an *"under-rower"* like one on the ancient battleship depicted in the movie *Ben-Hur.* Just as Paul viewed himself as a *bondservant,* when he said he was a servant of Christ, he also saw himself as an *under-rower.* This is another picture of what it means to have a true heart of a servant! Paul is saying that he is like one of these men under the ship, with no glory, no stature, no recognition, and no appreciation, yet faithfully rowing so the ship can successfully reach its destination.

The boat is like the church and its mission. An under-rower occupies a place of no recognition. It's the whole idea of doing things that are hidden with one goal in mind—get the boat to the destination. The people on top may even be singing, dancing, feasting, and having a great time, while not realizing all the hard work being done by those serving underneath. Of course, the Roman battleship had sails that caught the wind, which helped direct and empower the under-rowers. The sails represent the wind of the Holy Spirit which the under-rower must work in union with to reach the destination.

To be a servant of Christ is to care more about Christ and His church than anything else. It's to serve Him faithfully no matter the cost. As an under-rower, the view might not be great and the work may be difficult and tedious. There will be days when you will want to quit and not row one more inch; days that you are sick and tired of the oars God has assigned you to! Believe me. I had those days, and still have those days, where I want to just throw in the towel. My wife can tell you about them. On days like that, I've had to fall on my knees before God and cry out for the strength to take another step forward. If you are in ministry for any length of time, you will have those days too. After being tested again and again, you'll find out if you are serving from a pure heart or are simply doing works to be noticed.

When Ruth and I were helping with a church back in the 1980s, we were taught by men who had served as under-rowers. Today, I am so thankful for the hearts of these great leaders. They were truly servants. Early in the mornings on Sundays, we would get up and arrive at the rented building we used as the church while the rest of the people in the congregation were still sleeping. We would set up the chairs, sound equipment, and everything else needed for the service. Later that morning, everyone would come and have a great service. They would enjoy worship and have a good experience fellowshipping at church and then they would go back home. But we would stay for as long as it took to clean, pack up all the chairs, sound equipment, and return things to the way they were earlier that morning.

We worked long and hard so everyone else could enjoy a great church service. We were the under-rowers. Our hearts were to serve the ship and get the ship to where it needed to go. We were not looking for praise or recognition, but were serving because God had called us as servants. The people in the church were like those on the deck of the ship. They would enjoy the service and wouldn't think about who set up the chairs or got things ready for the service. They would come and have a great time, while the under-rowers were getting the ship to the place it needed to go.

Another time, Ruth and I were training people for missions in the local church. We both worked full-time jobs, yet we were doing this as servants because we knew God had called us. So, we would come in on Friday nights when no one was there and make all the copies of the mission manuals for each student. There were no personal computers back then and we had to prepare the material and print one page at a time. Sometimes we got to go home and catch a few hours of sleep before having to come back early in the morning to teach the class. Often, we would stay at the church all night.

God was training us to be under-rowers. Nobody knew the work we were putting in. We weren't doing it for recognition, but so those we were discipling could get to the destination God was calling them. *Under-rowers have their eyes fixed on the destination rather than the circumstances and environment.* Our number one destination should be to become like Him! Hudson Taylor once said, "If I would not allow anything to get in between Jesus and me, then every circumstance and pressure can only push me closer to His bosom." Birthed out of our personal relationship with Jesus, we are all called to become a servant of His church in some way, helping it reach its destination.

It is good to ask yourself about your motivation when you are serving in ministry. What would you do if no one recognizes you? Would you quit? This can be a *heart* test. A true under-rower will keep serving because their goal is seeing the church become more like the purified bride of Christ, even when no one notices. When I travel around the world and speak, rarely does anyone know all the work Ruth and I put into it and the things we do to leave one area and prepare for the next. The truth is, they don't need to know. We do it because we have learned to be under-rowers.

Early in my ministry, I didn't understand this concept and definitely didn't understand what it meant to have the *heart* of a servant. I was a slave focusing on performance and reward, not on my Master Jesus' desire. When God began to stir my heart for ministry, I knew he was calling me to China, but thankfully, as an act of His mercy, He didn't let me go there right away. He sent me to Estonia first!

God knew that my motivation was based on performance and achievement and that my confidence was in my own strength rather than His. So, He sent me to Estonia. I thought I was going to change Estonia, but God would use Estonia to change me. Pastor Rei would be one of God's instruments in Estonia to teach me to become an under-rower. After those first two weeks, I wound up spending about six years with him, submitted to his authority. Although I had learned many things in America, like how to teach, preach, and prophesy, I hadn't learned the most important things—how to have the heart of a true servant and to be an under-rower.

Early Days in Ministry

God knows our hearts and I'm so grateful that He changed mine. In the early days of ministry, I was blind to my own slave mentality. During that time, my church was part of a network and I was one of the top leaders. Within the network was an apostolic father who often visited our church. Like his shadow, I wanted to be as close to him as possible, soaking up as much wisdom and understanding as I could. He had decided to choose two young people from the network to train as key leaders. Of course, I wanted to be one of the two, so I did my best. The problem was, the competitive mode consumed me and I was driven to receive top recognition. There was another young man who was also being considered and this apostolic leader would always promote both of us to speak at churches within the network. Rather than feeling humbled and honored that he saw God's calling on my life, I became puffed-up with pride. Oh, I sounded humble, but in reality, I wanted to be the top man. I did not have the heart of an under-rower. My eyes were zeroed in on my competition.

Instead of building up my brother in the Lord and wishing him well, I was set on outshining him. When both of us spoke at conferences, I wanted to speak in the evening sessions because those sessions had the bigger crowds. As soon as the conference schedule came out, I would look to see who had the evening time slot. Because I felt I had the gifting and anointing, I also felt like I deserved to be the evening speaker. If he got to speak in the evening instead of me, I would get incensed! Being thankful and honored to just speak at the conference never crossed my mind. I could only focus on why he was assigned to speak in the evening and I was assigned to the morning when half the people had to work and couldn't even show up! I knew I could speak as well as he could, *even better*. I had a slave mentality and didn't even know it. But God knew it. He knew my heart all along. Yet, instead of tossing me aside or giving up on me, in His mercy, He sent me to Estonia to teach me how to be an under-rower.

In Estonia, I was hardly noticed by anyone and it felt like everybody in America had forgotten about me. In my forties, I was ministering to a small group of seniors, most in their seventies and eighties. I remember thinking, *I could be speaking to thousands of people in America, but here I am speaking to elderly ladies!* I was angry at my spiritual leadership in America for agreeing to send me to Estonia.

When I first arrived, I had an entitlement mentality and was used to performing for a reward. But in Estonia, I never received any reward. As I was serving, I spent a lot of time feeling frustrated. I kept thinking, *"Poor me, poor, pitiful, me!"* It felt like I was invisible, rowing with all my might below the deck. In reality however, I wasn't invisible to God who was faithfully at work in my life. Little by little, row by row, He was changing my heart. It took a while to realize Pastor Rei was teaching me to be an under-rower. In fact, it took several years and many difficult lessons for God to work the performance mentality out of me.

An Audience of One

One of the key lessons I learned in Estonia, that is at the heart of an *under-rower*, was to seek to please God, not man—to serve for an audience of One. That One is God. It doesn't matter what people think or even how much of us they see. What matters is what God thinks and sees. God sees our hearts. He knows our motives. Every single soul is precious to Him and should be to us. He wants us to begin to see *all* people with His eyes and love them the way He loves them. *"Assuredly, I say to you,"* declared Jesus, *"inasmuch as you did it to one of the least of these My brethren, you did it to Me"* (Matthew 25:40). Jesus wanted me to serve Him by serving the least of them, whether I received recognition or not. Pleasing Him is enough. But learning this lesson took time.

In Estonia, very seldom did people give compliments to others. In their language, the common adjective they had was "normal."

"How's your marriage?"

"Normal," they'd reply.

"How was your meal?"

"Normal."

I preached in many locations and often several times each week. Sometimes after I finished a sermon, wanting praise and recognition, I would ask Pastor Rei, "How did I do?" He would usually reply, "Normal." I had a hard time hearing that! I still had a slave mentality and was getting my worth and value from my accomplishments rather than from knowing I was simply God's servant. One day, I asked Pastor Rei how to deal with preaching time after time without anyone patting me on my back, saying how well I'd done. I'll never forget his response. "Brother, if the word is from God, it is always good regardless of how people respond."

That conversation affected me deeply and from that point on I looked at things differently. It didn't matter if I pleased man or not, even leaders in the church. What mattered was what God thought. Was I being obedient to what He told me to preach? I was to serve for an audience of One. If I preached at a church and wasn't invited a second time, I still would not compromise the Word of God. We are not to preach simply to make people feel warm and fuzzy. We preach God's Word because it is Truth and comes from Him.

Hebrews 4:12 tells us, *"For the word of God is living and powerful, and sharper than any two-edged sword, piercing even to the division of soul and spirit, and of joints and marrow, and is a discerner of the thoughts and intents of the heart."* Our sermons should be filled with the Word of God. A minister of the gospel is not out to win a popularity contest, but to present God's truth. Sometimes God's Word cuts. Sometimes it brings comfort. Sometimes it encourages. Which one is determined by the Holy Spirit, not us. Pastor Rei was an example to me in his love for God and his uncompromising commitment to Truth. He taught me to have the heart of an under-rower and to focus on serving for an audience of One.

The Obedient Under-Rower

Some things you just can't learn through a book or manual. They must be learned by experience. As we discover how to be God's under-rowers, one of the difficult lessons we will learn is how to be obedient. One night, someone broke into our apartment and stole everything we had of value. There was shattered glass and the door was smashed in. I was distraught and swimming in a pool of self-pity, but I had already committed to take Pastor Rei's old van and drive a group to another area of Estonia for ministry the next day. Knowing the importance of keeping my commitment, I set my concerns about the robbery aside, loaded up the dilapidated van, and began the long drive. This van was so old and had so many engine problems that it sputtered along the way. At one point, I thought it was so slow I could probably outrun it on foot. A few hours into our trip, the rickety van broke down. While we were able to get it fixed, a trip that should have only taken three hours took us eight!

After pouring out our hearts in ministry, we reloaded the van for the return trip. Completely exhausted, we finally rolled back home around two o'clock in the morning. Pastor Rei had asked me to return the van to his house as soon as we got back that night. I thought because it was so late and wanting to be considerate, I would just return the van in the morning. After all, we had just returned from an exhausting ministry trip and I was still processing the recent robbery of our apartment. Ruth and I were just crawling into bed, finally about to get some sleep, and there was a knock at our door. A young man from our ministry team told me Pastor Rei wanted his van back. I knew I was in trouble for not taking it back right away, so for moral support, my wife went with me to return it. As we pulled into his driveway, Pastor Rei was standing at the gate waiting. I told him that I was sorry and began to explain my reasons for not returning the van right away.

While talking with him, Ruth was in the car praying in the Spirit because she knew I had a temper and how frustrated I was about his insistence that the van be returned that night. Because of all I'd been through it took everything within me to hold back from an emotional outburst. After explaining my reasons for not bringing him the van, he said, "Brother, I wanted to tell you, maybe yesterday you got robbed because God is teaching you a lesson to be obedient." When he said this, I could feel the smoke coming out of my hair and the steam boiling inside me! I had just about had it! I thought to myself, *"I just got robbed . . . the van broke down on us . . . we have been driving all day . . . I had good intentions not to disrupt your sleep . . . so out of my best intentions, I decided to wait until the morning . . . and now this is what I get in return!"* I was so upset and I could feel my flesh rising up. I am convinced it was God answering my wife's prayers that I had the grace to keep my mouth closed. I took a hard, long swallow and said, "Pastor Rei, I'm sorry." I then walked quietly back to the car.

When I got back in the car, I was so upset I could hardly speak. Knowing my bad temper and propensity to explode, Ruth was wise and didn't say anything. She just put her hand on my shoulder, stayed quiet, and comforted me with her soft touch. She allowed the Holy Spirit to minister to me. Growing up, I had always fought for my rights. If I encountered an injustice, something in me would rise up to defend myself. I couldn't stand being treated unfairly. But in this moment, God was giving me the grace to just let it go. God was using this situation to help me die to my flesh because He wanted this area in my life to die.

A dead man would not stand up and defend his rights. A dead man wouldn't react in anger. God had brought me to Estonia to teach me that an under-rower does not have to defend himself like a slave. As I drove home and processed what God was doing in my heart, I knew He was teaching me to lay down my rights and let Him be my defender. He is faithful to take up our cause. We must learn to trust Him. Vengeance belongs to the Lord. The gentle voice of the Holy

Spirit told me to *be still* and *just obey.* Then the Holy Spirit dropped into my spirit, *"It doesn't matter how people treat you. That's not what you need to focus on. What you need to focus on is if you make a commitment, then you live up to the covenant even if it hurts, even if you have been mistreated."* After receiving that, I totally calmed down.

Two weeks later, Pastor Rei came to our house to celebrate our American holiday of Thanksgiving. I had already released the situation to the Lord and I didn't have any grudges in my heart. While we were talking that evening, Pastor Rei said to me, "Brother, I'm sorry about the other night. What happened caused me to think. Many people in the past have obeyed me because they know my personality is very strong. They would obey, but their hearts were not submitted. They were going through the motions on the outside, but inside, they were just waiting for their time. They would use me as a stepping stone to get to wherever they wanted to go. When they didn't need me anymore, they would trample me. The other night, not only did you obey, but you showed your love for me because you submitted. Brother, you are teaching me something."

"No problem," I told him.

And then he said, "Brother, I began to see from you what true loyalty is."

I was so blessed by his words, but more importantly, I had learned a valuable lesson. When we have a submissive heart,

God will always vindicate. I don't always have to take matters into my own hands. Many of us say we die to ourselves, but then we react to a situation in our flesh two minutes later. Did we really die to ourselves? We may have had a quick moment of obedience, but we never fully surrendered—our flesh never died. You will never learn obedience until you die and cut off the flesh. An under-rower doesn't defend himself, but is fully submitted to God.

Denying Self

God knew that one day I would become a spiritual leader in Asia so He continued to train me to have the heart of an under-rower during my time in Estonia. I still, however, had relationships with several ministries in America. So, as you can imagine, I was incredibly excited when I received an invitation to travel back home to be a keynote speaker at a major conference. Like a little kid wanting to impress their kindergarten teacher, I would repeatedly tell Pastor Rei about my opportunity to be a keynote speaker. Yet, his response was always the same—an indifferent, unenthusiastic, "Praise God." I was never able to get more affirmation out of him than that.

One month before I was to leave, I became very ill. It was a long, drawn-out sickness and when the time came for me to travel, I still had a fever, no energy, and felt depleted and discouraged. Originally, I was excited about my opportunity to be a conference speaker. Now, I just wanted to crawl back in bed and pull the covers over my head! But I couldn't do that. Not only was Ruth going, but I had invited Pastor Rei so he could come and see how *great* I was. I wanted him to see how much God had used me. I had served so faithfully doing the simple tasks in Estonia and I wanted him to know he had a high-quality preacher on his team!

We finally arrived in America the night before I was scheduled to preach. Still sick, I was running a fever. My head was throbbing and I was weak with a runny nose. Needless to say, I looked quite a mess. Yet I was supposed to preach at 9:00 a.m. the next morning. I was so frustrated at myself and discouraged—then I was mad at God. *"God,"* I thought to myself, *"how could you let this happen? I have a huge opportunity to let Pastor Rei see what a great speaker I am and now look at me! I'm a mess!"* As I was lying there in my self-pity, Pastor Rei walked in. He knelt before my bed, grabbed me by the arm and said, "No matter what you do tomorrow, remember God always loves you." Then he prayed Psalm 23 over me.

The next morning, with little energy and my head still fuzzy, I put on my suit. Mustering up everything in me, I determined that I was going to preach with all my heart. At 9:00 a.m. just as scheduled, I stepped up to the pulpit with

700 pastors looking at me. I had prepared a message that would have been popular to preach, but at that moment the Lord asked me to change my message to *Deny Yourself.* I could feel the Holy Spirit empowering me to speak. As you can imagine, this wasn't a standard message taught in the American pulpit—you could hear a pin drop.

As the pastors in the auditorium sat there listening, I could see Pastor Rei on the second row with a big smile on his face. As soon as I finished preaching, he was the first one to stand up and begin clapping. One by one, each pastor in the room stood up as the applause began to build. Although the message wasn't something I knew people heard from the pulpit very often, I knew God had anointed me in that moment—as I was denying my own flesh just to speak—to bring a word to leaders in the church.

God wants all of us to pick up our cross and follow Him—to be an under-rower for Christ. I learned from that moment on, I needed to walk in a way that was worthy of His calling by denying myself. I also experienced knowing that God loved me not because of my performance, but because I was His. Looking back at my time in Estonia, I am so thankful for everything God did in my heart; and I am so thankful He removed my slave-mentality and replaced it with the heart of an under-rower.

To answer the call of God on our lives, we must be like one of the men under the ship: with no glory, no stature, no recognition, and no appreciation, yet faithfully rowing so the ship can successfully reach its destination. The boat is like the church and becoming the bride of Christ is the final destination. As an under-rower, the view might not always be great, and the work may sometimes be hard and tedious. But to be a servant is to care more about Christ than anything else and to serve Him faithfully no matter the cost!

Questions for Reflection

1. If it were God's will for you to serve Him undetected, unnoticed, and unrecognized by others for the rest of your life, would you be willing?

2. Where would you find *joy* and *fulfillment* as an under-rower if there was no visible appreciation or recognition?

3. How would you grow in the ministry if you were not promoting yourself?

4

THE AVAILABLE HEART

"I thank Christ Jesus our Lord, who has given me strength, that he considered me trustworthy, appointing me to his service."

—1 Timothy 1:12 NIV

The blustery wind blew cold chills through my body as I weaved my way through the parking lot to the front entrance of the prison. Slowly, I continued past the chain-link fence and barbed-wire to the first security checkpoint. After checking my guitar case to make sure I didn't have any weapons or contraband, the guards led me through a dark corridor. Though I was a free man, I could feel the eerie surroundings closing in around me. Once past each security checkpoint, I was ushered into a room where I nervously waited. Soon, another door creaked open and more than thirty, hard-eyed African American prisoners filed into the room. As they eased their bodies into the empty metal chairs, they were surprised to see a small, obviously nervous, Chinese man standing before them.

As an Asian immigrant, I didn't understand many aspects of American culture or African American culture. Both cultures have a way of communicating and relating that was foreign to me. Now, here I stood at the front of the room, a foreigner in a foreign land. Wiping my brow with my sweaty palms, I thought, *"How in the world am I going to relate to these guys? I am from a completely different culture. I don't have a clue what I'm going to say."*

As I looked around the room, my mouth froze shut for several moments, creating an awkward silence. Then, a big man who had his feet propped up on the chair in front of him said something derogatory and they all started laughing at me. I was already feeling uncomfortable, but now my legs began to shake and my breaths became short. In that moment of crisis, I silently cried out to God, *"Lord, help me. I don't know what to do, but I know You love these men. Use me to minister to them. Show me what to say."*

Suddenly, the power and peace of God fell upon me. My mind quit racing and my breathing steadied. The Bible promises that when we call upon the Lord, the Holy Spirit will be faithful to help us and to answer us in our time of need, even in that moment called "embarrassment." *"For the*

Holy Spirit will teach you at that time what needs to be said" Luke 12:12 (NLT). Ephesians 6:10 reads, *"A final word: Be strong in the Lord and in his mighty power"* (NLT).

As I continued to inwardly cry out to the Lord in my moment of embarrassment, Bruce Lee popped into my mind. He was a hero of mine during the 1970s and I thought he was amazing. I began to talk about him and act out scenes from some of his movies. Then, I started imitating the way they talked in Bruce Lee's martial arts movies where their lips are moving, but they're not synced to the voices. That did it! It broke the ice. The prisoners sat up in their seats and tuned in to my message.

"Back in 1972," I told them, "Bruce Lee was my idol. I watched his movies and I admired the way he was such a great warrior. I admired how strong he was and I wanted to be just like him. He was lean and in perfect shape with almost no body fat. Then, in 1973, he unexpectedly died. Just like that, my idol was dead. I was so heartbroken, I cried. I was in shock; the man I idolized was gone. I struggled so much with his death, and as I did, I began to realize the value of what we live for. I thought to myself, *how good is it if a man gains the whole world but loses his soul?"* (Mark 8:36-37) As I finished talking, silence hung in the air.

The more I spoke and talked to these prisoners, the more they listened. God gave me courage and I could feel the Spirit of God surging through me. At the end I asked them, "How many of you are at a crossroad in your life and you find yourself going nowhere, just grabbing air?" As I shared and gave an opportunity for them to respond, all thirty-something of them came forward. Twenty-eight accepted Christ! For many of them it was not the first time they had heard the gospel. Others had shared the gospel with them, but when I gave the invitation, they responded. Afterward, we hugged and had a great connection. Some were so big I could barely get my arms around them. I came in as a foreigner, but left as a friend.

Just Say "Yes"

In the early days of our marriage, Ruth and I were hungry for God and for doing His work. God was beginning to teach us about being servants and we responded by making ourselves available and serving in many areas—short-term missions, worship, teaching, training, evangelism, and cell groups. Even though we both had full-time jobs, we were eager to serve wherever we could. The week our pastor asked for help in the prison ministry, I knew I needed to answer the call. Our church had ministered in the prisons for a while; however, the leadership struggled with getting people to volunteer. I decided not to make any excuses about not being involved in prison ministry. I simply said, "Lord, I'm available." This was my conviction, and that day in church, I timidly raised my hand to volunteer. Although the prison ministry was a foreign mission field to me, I was eager to serve the Lord and decided I would go. Because I made myself available and was willing to be uncomfortable, even embarrassed, God was able to use me to lead nearly thirty men to Christ. What a difference an *available* heart makes!

When you make yourself available—even in that moment of embarrassment or uncomfortableness—that is where Jesus will meet you. But as long as you stay safe in the boat, you will never experience God working through you. Just like Peter in the Bible, you must step out of the boat if you want to see the miracles happen—if you want to walk on the water. Ministering in the prison was the first assignment where I had an opportunity to preach. I stepped out of my boat of self-assurance and God showed me that I could preach. And I have been preaching ever since!

Also, as a testimony of God's grace, to this day I have a special connection with African Americans. I recently spoke to an African American mega-church and my topic was "slave or son." God has graciously used my Asian American heritage to allow me to minister cross-culturally, and I was able to share God's heart for my African American brothers and sisters. After my message, the pastor told me that God has given me a special grace to communicate cross-culturally.

Later, Ruth and I received a note from one woman who expressed she had never before heard that message on "slave or son" and it changed her life. She had been in bondage for seventy years, but God unlocked several things in her life during the message.

I have been so grateful for the opportunity I had that day in the prison and the difference it has made, not only in the lives of the prisoners that day, but also in my life. I simply made myself available. In the same way, you need to step out and be available. If you are willing to do the possible, God will do the impossible. Of course, God will not do what you are supposed to do, but will do what you cannot do. Don't be afraid to get out of the boat. Be willing, and God will use you to do great things! When Peter stepped out of the boat onto the sea, the storm was raging all around him. He responded to Jesus' call; although it looked like he would most likely drown. Yet, as Peter kept his eyes on Jesus, he walked on the water. As Jesus calls us to assignments larger than ourselves, we will do the impossible if we obey and keep our eyes fixed on Him.

Abraham and Eliezer

To be a great leader, availability is essential. Your greatest ability is your availability. It doesn't matter how gifted you are, if the trumpet sounds and you're not there, it doesn't do any good for anyone. The Bible is full of people who simply made themselves available to God and He used them to do great things.

I love the story in Genesis 24 about Abraham's servant Eliezer. He was a great servant who made himself available to his master. There are many lessons to be gleaned from the life of Eliezer. He was one of the first great servants we see in Scripture. God had promised that Abraham would be the father of many nations, yet at the time, his promised son, Isaac, wasn't even married. However, Eliezer was so trusted that Abraham asked him to find a wife for his son. Can you imagine the amount of faith Abraham had in him? Without a proper wife, Isaac would not have children and Abraham would never become the father of many nations.

Abraham knew Eliezer so well and had confidence that he would do a great job following the one simple instruction given—find Isaac a wife not among the Canaanites. That was it. Abraham's chief servant had to find a wife that would affect the entire life of Isaac. I love Eliezer's response to Abraham because he only had one question and it was a simple one— he only wanted to know if he could bring Isaac along. It was a simple conversation, both ways. Eliezer knew Abraham's heart and quickly answered Abraham's request through the woman of Rebekah.

As I have developed leaders in China, this relationship is a model for me. I want to be in close relationship with my leaders so that they know my heart, just like Abraham and Eliezer. I focus on developing the connection so that if God ever calls me home, I can simply tell them, "Go into China" and I would know the work would continue. A leader like Abraham must spend time with his or her disciples by being available for them. Likewise, a servant like Eliezer must be trustworthy, spend time learning the heart of their leader, and be available for any task. Both servant and leader must be available. Actually, the best leader is a servant-leader.

In a closer look at the relationship between Abraham and Eliezer, we see not only was Eliezer available to serve Abraham, but he also studied his master. A successful servant must be attentive in knowing his master for them both to be of one heart and one mind. A servant who knows his master makes a deep impact. In the same way, we must study Christ. As we study Christ and search the Scriptures, we will know God's ways and recognize His voice. When we know the voice of Christ, then all He must do is say, "Go" and we will know His heart. Jesus didn't give page after page of detailed strategy; much like Abraham didn't give pages of instructions to Eliezer. We need to know Jesus so well and know His ways so we can easily do His will without much explanation.

When we study our Master, we are ready to hear His still, small voice and we are ready to be available.

Actively Communicate

When you work for your leaders, make sure you ask the right questions and understand all the parameters before launching out into the deep. The servant (Eliezer) asked, "But what if I can't find a young woman who is willing to travel so far from home? Should I then take Isaac there to live among your relatives in the land you came from?" (Genesis 24:5 NLT). Eliezer asked about his parameters and then wisely chose his actions. He wanted to remain faithful to the directives given by his master. Yet, he also was proactive. In the same way, we must be proactive with our leaders. An available servant also asks about the vision so he or she can bring about the desired results. Active communication between you and your leader should continue until the project or ministry is complete. An available servant communicates when they're finished with the task. Don't be passive or assume your leader knows all the completed details. Being proactive on the front end to know expectations, and being proactive on the back end to communicate, will build trust with your leaders.

While we might know a servant should be available and actively communicate, a *wise* servant also responds from a pure heart, free of vainglory and selfish ambition. Eliezer had a pure heart. He was single-focused and single-purposed. Following one direction, he completed his work and returned home. Eliezer's interests remained pure. He didn't get side-tracked or do multiple things. No. He went and did the job, blessing his master.

Blessed to Be a Blessing

Do you desire to bless your leaders? Do you pray for your leaders? Are you single-focused like Eliezer was for Abraham? Eliezer humbled himself before he went on his journey. He prayed. He knew he needed God's help and wasn't prideful or overconfident in his own strength. When given a task or assignment, do we humble ourselves in this same way? Do we seek God before we do anything? When given an assignment, we should pray before we do anything. We should always pray first. Prayer cultivates a humble spirit—a servant dependent on God.

Even though he was the chief servant, Eliezer was dependent on God and asked God for help. He prayed for success, and prayed God would show loving-kindness toward his master. Eliezer had a heart to bless Abraham and to help him be successful. "'O Lord, God of my master, Abraham,' he prayed. 'Please give me success today, and show unfailing love to my master, Abraham'" (Genesis 24:12 NLT).

What is the real definition of success? *The only real success we can achieve is when we bless our leader and God is glorified.* Wow! My prayer for these last days is that God gives us more Eliezers!

Living in modern times, you may be thinking, *"Who is my master? Who am I serving?"* Well, as a believer, Jesus is our Master and we are His servants first and foremost. The only reason we want success is so that Jesus is glorified. If success only brings our own glory, it is not success. Jesus confirms this when He spoke, *"If any of you wants to be my follower, you must give up your own way, take up your cross, and follow me. If you try to hang on to your life, you will lose it. But if you give up your life for my sake and for the sake of the Good News, you will save it. And what do you benefit if you gain the whole world but lose your own soul? Is anything worth more than your soul?"* (Mark 8:34-37 NLT).

We want to succeed so God is glorified and His Kingdom is expanded. We want to bless our Master. Pray for success so God is glorified. And when God grants you success, glorify your Master! King David echoes this truth in Psalm 115:1, *"Not to us, LORD, not to us, but to your name be the glory, because of your love and faithfulness"* (NIV).

Success also means that when we are loyal to our leader, we are also loyal to his designated leader. "Then Rebekah lifted her eyes, and when she saw Isaac she dismounted from her camel; for she had said to the servant, 'Who is this man walking in the field to meet us?' The servant said, 'It is my master. . .'" (Genesis 24:64-65). Why would the oldest servant of his house, who ruled over all, call Isaac "my master" when Abraham was his master before he embarked on the journey? When the servant is loyal to his master, he is also loyal to his master's designated successor. I believe the same loyalty and availability that Eliezer had toward Abraham was also modeled before his son, Isaac.

Long ago, in Jewish culture, the chief servant would raise the first child. He would train the child (almost like a slave) so he would learn all the responsibilities. Raising a son in this manner ensured he knew all the details of keeping up with the estate. Learning as a slave under the direction of the chief servant gave the child the perspective to be a good leader when he came of age. At that time, he would receive the inheritance of sonship. The son, although raised as a servant, would one day inherit the estate. When the son inherited the estate, he would have the character of a chief servant. He would be available, attentive, single-focused, and desire the success of the master. With this biblical imagery in mind, Romans 8 talks about the Spirit of adoption and becoming heirs with Christ—the Master of all.

Many times, we miss these simple principles in our lives. *We don't like training as a carpenter's son, but we want to do the work of a Messiah!* Sadly, this is why people get ahead of themselves. And this is why a superstar ends up as a falling star—because they never went through the training process. The chief servant would train the son so the son would have the correct heart. If God ever trusts us with His estate, we will first have to be trained by one of his chief servants of the estate. If we try to skip this principle, we will easily become caught up with vainglory, fame, selfish ambition, and the glories of the estate rather than the glories of our Master.

Free to Be Me

The day I stood in the prison facing those men was a turning point for me. However, this moment and my availability would never have happened if I had not first discovered who I am in Christ (i.e. sonship). You see, we can only receive freedom and courage when we connect with our Creator and we know who we are in Him. I felt bold enough to raise my hand and volunteer because I knew that I was God's son and a co-heir with Christ, our Bridegroom. No matter where I went, He would go before me—He would be there with me. If I had allowed myself to give in to self-doubt and self-condemnation, I would have never left my house that day. Was I nervous? You bet. Yet, I also knew who I was in Christ. I knew the great Carpenter, Jesus, who had wonderfully crafted me.

I have two cousins, both with biblical names. Growing up, both were taller, smarter, and more handsome than I was, and my aunt would always tell me I was ugly and stupid. I always wore hand-me-down clothes and was judged and overlooked because of my appearance. My cousins were well-groomed and had a great appearance on the outside. But even though they had all the makings of being great, and were even named after powerful biblical men, today neither of them are believers, and now they have lost their good looks too! They look so much older than I do (serving Jesus keeps you looking young). Unfortunately, my cousins are serving money and serving the world.

Never let people speak negative things to you, look down on you, or judge you. Know your identity in Christ. With that as your bedrock, you can serve God regardless of insults thrown your way. Jesus was sworn at, humiliated, and mocked, but He was still the Son of God. Boldness, courage, freedom, and confidence come when you know who you are in Christ!

To be rooted and grounded in Christ, you must hold on to God's Word and remember that Psalm 139 says you are fearfully and wonderfully made. When God made you, He said, "It is good." When you are looking at someone else and want to be like them and do things like them, you are missing God's unique plan and purpose. God grieves when

His creation isn't living out their divine purpose and they want to mimic someone else. Stop the cycle of envy, jealousy, and comparison. God made you. You are His son and daughter. Once you are free and you know you are a child of the Creator, other people's words don't mean as much because you know who you are. When you know your identity, you won't complain when God has you in training. You won't become disheartened when you are learning to work as the son and daughter of the Carpenter.

Questions for Reflection

1. Has it ever occurred to you that your greatest ability is your availability? If not, what are some things that may hinder you from believing this truth and getting involved: pride, lack of faith, complacency?

2. Who is really your true master? Are you fully available to Christ for total obedience at any cost?

3. Do you really know who you are in Christ? Do you find yourself fully content at all times, regardless of what you have or have not accomplished in the eyes of others?

5

PUREN

"Serve one another humbly in love."

—Galatians 5:13 NIV

Have you ever wondered what it would be like to meet a leader of five-million people? *How would they dress? What type of car would they drive? What would their official title or name be?* Many ideas and images might pop into your mind, but from firsthand experience, I can tell you that the answer can be surprising.

During the 1990s, Ruth and I were just beginning our work and ministry with the "house churches" in China. Of course, it is illegal to have any type of Bible school or Bible training for leaders without first registering with the government. We were blessed to have begun speaking and teaching in the house churches and we loved serving the leaders there.

Early in our ministry training, it came to our attention that there was one main overseer of this secret network of churches and their leaders. The network consisted of about five-million people. This leader was spoken of often, but never by name. Just as the network of churches were secret, so was his identity. One day, after one of my training sessions, I asked some of the church leaders gathered in the meeting who this overseer was. *"Puren,"* was their reply again and again.

This didn't make any sense to me because I knew the translation for this mandarin word was *servant.* I was looking for a specific name of a man. So, I continued asking, "What is the name of your leader? Who is he?" Again, the reply was, *"Puren."* Finally, I asked them, "Why do you keep saying the word *Puren*, which means servant?" The young man speaking with me explained that in China when someone has served Christ faithfully over a long period of time and when they have suffered for Christ and oversee millions of people, we give them the highest honor and title of all, *Puren*, which translates *servant.* I was surprised at their answer and even more surprised when it didn't appear that I would be able to meet this man.

Time passed, and during the next year, the leaders in the house church network attended my trainings and increased in their faith in God. They also grew to trust me as a leader because they experienced firsthand that I was a true follower of Christ and that my teachings were based completely on the Bible. One day, after one of my training sessions, some of the leaders approached me with the possibility that I might be able to meet the *Puren*. They told me that they couldn't guarantee anything, but they would contact me later with more details.

As the Lord would have it, the day came when I was given the opportunity to meet the top leader of this network of five-million people. Excited and nervous, I wasn't sure what to expect. Interestingly, I was informed the meeting would take place in a large city—to go there, get a hotel room, and wait for further instructions. They would be driving in from a different city and would contact me when they were close. Just like they promised, when the time arrived, I was told to go to a certain public area and they would find me. Soon, an extremely small minivan pulled up to where I was standing and a man jumped out and instructed me to jump in. I recognized the man as one of the leaders that had attended my trainings, so I felt comfortable following his orders. The Chinese word given for this type of minivan means *loaf of bread*. I felt like this was significant because Jesus was born in Bethlehem, which translates as the place of bread, and Jesus is the bread of life. And in the same way, this man—*Puren*—was bringing the love and teachings of Jesus to a network of five-million people.

Five men were cramped inside, but none of them seemed agitated or uncomfortable. As soon as the door shut, the van sped off down the street and we began driving all around the city. For this leader to evade arrest by the Chinese police, the driver needed to make sure the van was constantly on the move. Scanning the faces in the van, I had little problem identifying the *Puren*. Not because of how he was dressed, because his outward adornment was plain in an effort to avert attention from himself. No, I knew who he was from the weightiness that exuded from his presence and because of the honor and reverence the other men gave him. If you saw him on the street, nothing would stand out about him except Christ-likeness.

This man, the leader of a network of more than five-million people, was kind, gentle, soft-spoken, polite, humble, eager to learn, and just as excited to meet with me as I was to meet with him. His loyal and faithful team revered him as he had suffered much over the years leading the network of house churches. For nearly two hours, he and I discussed how to build the church, all while the van was in motion. We talked about the foundation of the church, its vision, and specific strategies. Though twenty years my senior, he was eager to hear my thoughts and ideas. There was no sense of competition or arrogance, only humility and honor.

At the end of our time together, the minivan pulled up to the spot where they had originally picked me up. After expressing my gratitude for our time together, they dropped me off. On my way back to the hotel room, I knew that something special had occurred. I would never be the same. This brief encounter had made a significant impact on my heart and mind. I was moved by how the *Puren* was so Christ-like. He was humble, meek, gentle, and excited to be with others. This important experience helped shape my future perspective of ministry and my beliefs about what significance in God's Kingdom really looks like.

Diakonos Training

Because of the encounter with such a great man who was called *Puren*, I began to look into the word servant and servanthood to understand the man and how he had such a great influence. I understood that the function of a deacon in the church has a lot to do with "serving" and being a servant. In 1 Timothy 3:8, Paul writes about the qualifications for deacons, those who serve the church. The Greek word he uses for deacon is *diakonos*. This word, translated deacon here, can also be defined as a servant such as one who waits on tables or serves food. A *diakonos* is one who serves by doing menial tasks.

When in college, I worked at a nice Chinese restaurant where I learned what it means to be this kind of a servant. There was a master waiter who had been there for many years and trained all the new waiters. I didn't realize at the time, but what he taught us was a perfect spiritual application of the term *diakonos*. He taught three main keys that were important to be a successful waiter.

First: When you serve people, you should always be in the standing position while they are in the sitting position. When you are standing, you can see much better than if you are sitting. I had to work twelve hours a day and rarely sat down. As difficult as that was at the time, and as much as I disliked standing for so long, that training was critical to my future as a minister. Today in many countries, I stand twelve hours a day when teaching.

Also, when you are standing as a waiter, or as a *diakonos*, you are mobile. You can move easily and respond quickly to the needs of others. We are serving God not just by being available, but by being mobile and accessible to others. I let my people know that I'm a phone call away. In my mind and practically, I'm always in a standing position in order to be ready to respond as quickly as possible. Ruth and I sold our car and got rid of much of our stuff so we could be more mobile for ministry. I have found that people can become too attached to things. Sometimes their attachment to things causes them to be less mobile, or less responsive to the people they are serving. God wants our hearts to be in a standing position so we are ready and available to respond.

Second: We were instructed to keep our eyes on the customer. When waiting, I would stand so I could see my tables and see the customers. My focus was on them. In the same way, our eyes should always be focused on Jesus. When we are looking to Him, He will give us His heart for the people He has called us to serve. We can then focus on serving those to whom we have been sent. Jesus said that as much as we have done for the least of these, we have done unto Him (Matthew 25:40). Therefore, as we are serving them, we are serving Jesus. When our eyes are attentive to the people we are serving, and we are in a standing position, we will be better prepared to meet their needs.

At a restaurant, when a person needs water, they look for their waiter. But if the waiter is looking attentively, he will see and notice when the water gets low and will fill it up even before they ask. Can you imagine if every leader had this type of attentiveness and a servant's heart for people? When our eyes are on them and we take care of the least of these, we are serving as a *diakonos*.

Third: The master waiter taught us that a good waiter was to be in a hiding place. Have you ever been to a restaurant where you're trying to have a deep conversation, but the waiter keeps interrupting? We were taught that, although our eyes were fixed on the table, we ourselves were to remain invisible and watch from a distance so we didn't interrupt at the wrong time. We would wait in a standing position, with our eyes on the table, in a hidden place, ready for when the customer needed us.

It is the same way in ministry. We are to remain in the secret place and not the spotlight. This is similar to the way secret service agents are with the president. The secret service agents are hyper-attentive. They're aware of the president along with the people and environment around him. Yet, they themselves remain discreet, deflecting attention away from themselves. They are there, but are in a hidden place while the president is in the spotlight. When we serve, people should see God, not us. I watch people so I can help them, but I try to remain hidden. John the Baptist said, *"He must increase, but I must decrease"* (John 3:30 ESV). When we minister with a servant's heart, it is about humbling ourselves and bringing glory to God, not us. As we serve, our goal should be *diakonos*, serving as one who waits tables. This is the essence of a servant's heart.

As my partner in ministry and life, Ruth does so much to serve me. She has a quiet and gentle spirit and works hard behind the scenes. If anyone models the heart of a servant, it is Ruth. She has lived with me for more than twenty years in China and has served faithfully and quietly without any recognition. The whole time I've been working in China, I've had to be extremely clandestine. Because of the nature of our work and the fact that I've been arrested for preaching the gospel in the past, we aren't able to associate with other believers in our home city. I travel and do ministry all over China, but in the city where we live, we have to be disconnected from our work and ministry so we don't draw attention to ourselves.

Ruth isn't able to associate with missionaries, other foreigners in our city, or other house churches in our city. When we lived in a city of several million, we didn't realize how important it was for us to separate our ministry from our home city. One day, the Chinese police were knocking at my door because my life and ministry were interconnected. The Chinese police are always looking for suspicious persons or activities. Because they track all foreigners, we can't have casual interactions with them or we put the work of the ministry at risk. I do all my church planting and raising up leaders in other cities, but not my own.

It doesn't matter our country, city, or profession, God has called us to do the work of servants, wherever we are. If God had not sent me to Estonia before He sent me to China, I would not have developed a servant's heart. Before my time in Estonia, I would do ministry as a notch on my belt, a trophy, or as a stepping stone for promotion. While serving under Pastor Rei, however, God used the difficult circumstances to develop the heart of a servant in me. He will use difficult circumstances to develop a servant's heart in you too.

Not Called to Preach, but to Obey

In Estonia, we had bitterly cold winters. There were times the temperature got down below zero! Additionally, because it used to be a communist country, there were times during those cold winters where stores had nothing on their shelves except a little cheese and a little bread. Imagine going into your local Wal-Mart and the shelves were empty save a few loaves of bread, some cartons of eggs, and cheese. It's hard for us in America to wrap our minds around that scenario, yet it was a reality in Estonia. It was difficult to get anything outside the bare necessities. Even gasoline was scarce. I have vivid memories of long lines of cars at the pumps waiting hours to get a little petrol. Some would even sleep in their car all night at the station. You would see their windows fogged up with ice, as they were in their freezing car, shivering under a blanket. They would have to scrape the ice off their windows on the inside and the outside just so they could see. Now that is cold!

One time I had to get five gallons of gas because we had to travel to another area for ministry. We had a Mitsubishi van that was about fifteen years old. So, in the dead of winter, I woke up while it was still dark in order to wait in line. It was bitterly cold and I was wrapped in a blanket in my car. After waiting more than seven hours in the freezing cold, I finally couldn't stand it any longer. "God!" I cried out. "I thought you called me to preach! But here I am in this long line waiting for hours just to get a little gas! I am wasting my time and I'm not preaching to anyone! What's going on here?" Right then, I heard God's still, small voice speak ever-so-clearly to my heart. *"Son, I didn't call you to preach. I called you to obey."* Wow! God lovingly but sternly reminded me of my true ministry and adjusted my heart. Obedience is always better than sacrifice. God has called us first and foremost, to obey. Before we can truly do the *serving* work, we must have the heart of a servant. That is what God has called us to.

When you have the heart of a servant, it doesn't matter if you are pumping gas or preaching to thousands. You are serving for an audience of One. This can be hard to do because we live in such a competitive world. Everybody is trying to get ahead of somebody else. All too often people will be promoted based on gifts and talents rather than character. While gifts and talents are important, unless they are submitted to Christ and His character, they mean nothing. Our cry should be, "Lord, less of me, more of You. Use me. Serve through me. Love through me."

God's Kingdom is not based on us exalting our gifts and talents, but on serving others. The character of Jesus is having a servant's heart. *"Let this mind be in you which was also in Christ Jesus, who, being in the form of God, did not consider it robbery to be equal with God, but made Himself of no reputation, taking the form of a bondservant, and coming in the likeness of men. And being found in appearance as a man, He humbled Himself and became obedient to the point of death, even the death of the cross"* (Philippians 2:5-8). The more Christ-like we become, the more of a servant we will become.

It's not how much knowledge you have. It's what's in your heart that matters. If you are in ministry, ask yourself, "Do I minister out of a servant's heart? Do I love these people like Jesus does, or do I just want a platform to preach? Am I here to serve, even without recognition or reward?"

When we have the heart of a servant, we are serving God simply because we love Him. We don't do it for money or for recognition. If God blesses us financially, or brings anything our way, it is just a *surprise*. It is an extra blessing. It is not an expectation. If we work hard and our boss recognizes us, it's a *surprise*. If I get a monetary raise at work, it is a *surprise*. If I ever get promoted to a higher position in ministry, it too is a *surprise*. With this mindset, our hearts stay humble. My expectation is that I'm just a servant giving back because God has done so much for me, including dying on a cross. God is searching for men and women who will serve Him like this, servants who will follow Him because of love!

Questions for Reflection

1. What if your highest title in life was called "servant?" Would you be content and not strive for anything else?

2. What does being a servant look like for you?

3. How did the stories in this chapter challenge your thoughts about servanthood?

6

THE LOYAL HEART

"Commit your way to the Lord; trust in him and he will do this: He will make your righteous reward shine like the dawn, your vindication like the noonday sun."

—Psalm 37:5-6 NIV

At ten-years-old, I had been trained in taekwondo and martial arts. Not only was I able to fight, but many people were scared of me and I liked that. It made me feel powerful. Tough as nails, I wasn't afraid to retaliate or avenge myself. My philosophy and mindset in life was, "An eye for an eye and a tooth for a tooth. If you offend me, I will avenge myself and my honor!"

So there I was, a ten-year-old fighter walking into my fourth grade classroom, when I noticed two boys bigger than me holding my bookcase, smirking. They were bullies and when they saw me, they threw my bookcase to the ground daring me to do something about it. Instead of cowering back in fear, rage came over me. My eyes blazed. *How dare you do that to my bookcase!* I thought as I walked up to them, squaring them up. I reached down, picked up their books, and dumped them on the floor. Then I began to jump up and down on them. The whole time my eyes were fixed on them in anger, expecting them to show me some respect, but they only laughed at me.

When I looked down at the books under my feet, I noticed they were mine! I was trampling my own books! My face turned bright red as I realized they had switched the books. They had only knocked my bookcase on the floor. This may not seem like a big deal to many, but to me it was huge. I was humiliated, and the experience would impact my future . . . and my pursuit of loyalty.

Twenty-Five Years Later

What comes to your mind when you read the word *loyalty?* Does the idea recall happy memories, or do you feel a strong sense of hurt or distrust? After decades of ministry, I have found that the godly principle of loyalty is a foundational element to building God's Kingdom on earth. We must understand it. However, I have also discovered that because of leaders who didn't walk in integrity or because many have been hurt by the church, there can be flare ups of negative emotions whenever principles of loyalty are taught. If people have not been healed of emotional wounds by the Holy Spirit, loyalty can be a difficult topic to discuss. I completely understand the challenge some may have with this, because I have experienced my own hurts from leadership. Yet, I've also learned that just because someone overseeing a local church makes a mistake, it doesn't discount the power that is released when God's people serve with loyal hearts.

For years, Ruth and I faithfully served our local church in America. Then in 1990 after already having completed multiple short-term mission trips to Estonia, the apostolic leadership at our church believed we were ready to pursue God's plan for our lives. As the leadership recognized God's anointing on our lives for ministry, they gathered around us to lay hands on us and send us out. Our short-term mission trips turned into an exciting move to Estonia to minister full-time.

In Estonia, we served Pastor Rei for several years, increasing in wisdom and knowledge. During that time, we became familiar with the culture, customs, and the likes and dislikes of the people. For anyone interested in serving internationally, it is essential to understand that when you go to a new country to serve a pastor, church, or ministry, you must always be sensitive to the customs and principles of that nation or people group.

Ruth and I continued to grow in our understanding of the cultural and church dynamics over the years we served in Estonia. One day however, after we had been there for a year, a short-term mission team came to minister. Ruth and I hosted and served as liaisons between them and the Estonian team. Since we had lived there for a while, we now had a better understanding of the Estonian culture and their approach to ministry. God had done a lot of work on me, and taught me how to serve the people and church as an under-rower. We honored Pastor Rei and the indigenous people by respecting their culture and the way they conducted ministry.

If a mission team travels to another country and doesn't have a servant's mindset or is not aware that they have a different relationship to the people in that culture, they will still act like they do back home. Like I did when I first came to Estonia, they may begin to command people and tell them what to do, unknowingly disrespecting their culture.

Anyone from the outside who wanted to minister in Estonia needed to be respectful of God's established leadership in that region. However, when the team from America came, several times they overstepped their boundaries and were commanding and overruling. As I watched, I saw it was beginning to negatively affect their ability to relate to the Estonian leadership and the people in the church. Recognizing they were out of bounds and disrespecting the leadership,

I approached the leader of the American team and gently said, "I know your heart is to do ministry and you are eager to serve, but in your zeal to serve, it's important to remember that this isn't our country. Here in Estonia, they do things differently than we do in America. They have different protocols here." I thought he would appreciate the feedback. Instead, he took offense. I knew both cultures and was trying to help bridge the gap, but that is not how he interpreted my words.

A few days later, we attended a beautiful appreciation dinner put on by the Estonian church. It was a big deal to them. The Estonians had put a lot of money into providing this dinner because they wanted to extend their gratitude and show honor. Using elegant place settings, they delicately set out the decorations, fresh flowers, candles, plates, and nice silverware. Because Pastor Rei was unable to attend, he delegated authority to me to lead the time together. I was at the end of the table with several Estonian pastors on one side and the team of Americans on the other side.

This was the type of dinner setting where the plates had covers over them and the hot meal was underneath. Before we began to eat, I had excused myself to the restroom. While away from the table, unbeknown to me and the Estonian pastors, someone on the American team decided to play a practical joke on me. When it came time to eat, we lifted the fancy covers off our plates and to my shock they had placed a dead mouse right on my plate! Some of the Americans started giggling and laughing, but none of the Estonians were laughing—to them what happened to me was very disrespectful. Not to mention, I was completely humiliated!

Here, I had the honor of running this meeting of leaders from both nations and this is when they decided to play their practical joke. We went on with our dinner and somehow I handled it gracefully. We finished the meal without further shaming the Estonian pastors or myself. It was hard for me though, because the whole time I was eating I couldn't stop thinking about the dead mouse . . . or about getting even. The events from being bullied as a ten-year-old erupted to the surface of my mind.

Afterwards, I confronted one of the leaders who had been giggling and laughing. I asked him why the dead mouse was so funny to him. I knew he was the one who had done it, and asked him if it was his idea. He admitted he did it, but it was another leader's idea. It was his way of humiliating me in front of everyone after I had approached him about his cultural mistakes in Estonia. He was getting me back. I knew I needed to just let it go. That was not the time or place to do anything. I was not mature enough at that time to properly process the emotional humiliation I experienced that night.

After the team left, thoughts about what happened replayed over and over again in my mind. I also kept thinking about all the problems of the trip and the way the team had shown cultural insensitivity and of course, disrespect. The more I pondered it, the more my frustration grew. I wanted to get them back for their disloyalty.

Instead of them receiving my rebuke and correction however, everything was turned against me and I was later the one accused of being disloyal. How could that even happen? It was so false and I was devastated. Even so, the Holy Spirit was present through it all and actually used this incident to cause me to reflect upon myself. I did some serious soul searching and asked the Lord about my own heart. This is what a *Puren*, under-rower does. It's what God was still teaching me. I had a long way to go. I had to learn to trust Him to defend me. Psalms 37:5-6 says, *"Commit your way to the LORD; trust in him and he will do this: He will make your righteous reward shine like the dawn, your vindication like the noonday sun"* (NIV). If there was any character flaw in me that would have the potential of hindering or even blocking my destiny, I needed to know. I wanted God to wash me and cleanse me of anything that wasn't pleasing to Him. I had been accused of disloyalty and now I needed to hear from God. What was *His* verdict? So, Ruth and I took time to seek God and just listen. Again, I was brought back to the bookcase incident when I was ten years old.

God revealed to me that I was living under the old commandment that said, "Eye for an eye and a tooth for a tooth." I still had the mindset that if you offended me, I would retaliate and avenge myself. This was the way I had always lived and throughout my life, I was proud when people were scared of me. Whenever I was in an unjust situation, I would respond in my flesh by fighting back. From ten years old to thirty-five years old, I was carrying the character flaw of *self-righteousness. "But we are all like an unclean thing, and all our righteousnessses are like filthy rags; we all fade as a leaf, and our iniquities, like the wind, have taken us away"* (Isaiah 64:6). No, I was not disloyal, but I had this issue in my life that God needed to deal with so I could further fulfill my destiny.

Healing the Brokenhearted

Many times, we go through life and wonder why people aren't relating well to us, or why we break relationships all the time, or hop from one church to another. Could it be that we are carrying something within us we don't realize? If a spiritual father would have seen my character flaw earlier, he would have mentored me, taught me, and helped me and I wouldn't have had to suffer for so long.

When God reminded me of the story when I was ten and how I had reacted to the mouse, it illuminated the character flaw in my flesh that I had previously been blind to. Jesus said in John 8:32, *"And you will know the truth, and the truth will set you free"* (NLT). In this moment of prayer, God was setting me free. When I see injustice, I fight it. The problem was: I was fighting in the *flesh*, not the *spirit*. Now, I was so grateful for the teaching of the Holy Spirit. I praised God and thanked Him for allowing that situation so I could see the real me. By His grace, He began to minister to me, deliver me, and do a deep work of healing in my heart. I have never been the same. Since then, people have wronged me, and rather than responding in my flesh with an "eye for an eye" mentality, I can respond by turning the other cheek. It was a supernatural work of the Holy Spirit. Certainly, I still struggle, but God dealt with my character at the roots, breaking the stronghold. *Even though I was loyal in my heart, I was walking in the flesh. But God wanted me to be loyal and walk in the Spirit!*

This is not the end of the story, though. Years later, a senior pastor from a large, influential congregation invited Ruth and me to be a part of an international team of twelve worldwide zone leaders, and he asked me to speak at one of the pastor's conferences. I spoke the Word to more than a thousand pastors and leaders. At the end of the service, the former leader who had instigated the mouse incident, came and found me. He was one of the pastors in the audience while I was speaking. He put his hand on my shoulder, looked me in the eyes and said, "Brother, I just want you to know I am very, very proud of you and Ruth." It is amazing how God works! God allowed us to reconcile with the leader who initiated the whole thing.

When I stopped fighting in my flesh, God fought for me in the Spirit. To this day, I don't have to fight for my rights. I was changed from being self-righteous to walking in God's righteousness. God brought about reconciliation and God was my defender. We always talk about our rights, but when we follow Jesus, we lay down our rights. We lay down defending ourselves. We are loyal to the Lord and loyal to the leaders God puts into our lives. Even though there are times leadership can hurt us, we can remain loyal to the Lord, knowing He is our defender. He is faithful.

Questions for Reflection

1. What *mission principle* stands out to you in this chapter?

2. Do you remain "loyal to the end," even when others accuse you of being disloyal?

3. After praying, has the Holy Spirit revealed any character flaws in your life? What behavior pattern is He
   showing you?

4. In what areas of your life are you fighting in the flesh
   instead of the Spirit?

5. Do you fight for your rights with your own strength, or
   do you rely on God?

7

LOYALTY IN ACTION

"As you also learned from Epaphras, our dear fellow servant,
who is a faithful minister of Christ on your behalf."

—Colossians 1:7

In the early 1990s, I was teaching this principle of loyalty
to a group of leaders in Hong Kong, but as I was speaking,
a riot almost broke out. There was a missionary there who
became so angry because of my teachings that he was ready
to throw stones at me! Many of the leaders gathered there
had been hurt by the church in the past and these hurts had
turned into festering wounds. Almost all of them had left
their local church at one point to do ministry on their own.
But because their wounds had never been dealt with properly,
they never received a breakthrough or healing. Ruth and I
were shocked to hear some of their stories. We had experienced hurt from our own local church, but we knew that just

because we had trouble didn't disqualify God's principle of loyalty in our lives.

Yes, it is true that sometimes people get hurt or disappointed by leadership. Leaders are human after all. Still, the local church is God's tool to bring His Kingdom on the earth. It is an incubator for people to grow in their walk with God and in their calling. The local church is the place where we are trained and nourished. It is God's design, and He uses the church to pour a spiritual foundation into our lives. Just because man messes up doesn't mean that God's institution is wrong. In the same way, just because there are some messed up families, or marriages that end in divorce, it doesn't disqualify God's institution of marriage. It doesn't mean I don't get married because there are some bad marriages out there.

God's design and system is right. Some people don't want to talk about loyalty because they've been hurt, but God calls us to have loyal hearts. I am loyally committed to the local church. I started out as a member, then became a deacon, an elder, and eventually, served our pastoral team full-time before being sent out as a missionary. In every role I've held in the local church, I've learned God is always loyal. *Loyalty is demonstrated through our consistent experiences of staying firm in our commitments over time.* Loyalty is also a heart issue. All of us experience difficulties, but I've seen first-hand that God can heal you and use whatever situation you are in to make you more like Christ.

Similarly, the biblical character Joseph never fought for his rights. As his story unfolds in Genesis, chapters 37-50, he was mistreated, falsely accused, and put into prison. Yet Joseph understood the principle of loyalty. As a result, God raised him up to become the second most powerful man in Egypt, right under Pharaoh. Joseph wasn't loyal to Pharaoh because he was godly or perfect. He was loyal because he trusted God. By faith, he believed everything that had happened to him was a part of God's design. This is the spirit of loyalty we need to catch.

Sometimes we have the idea that we will only be loyal to a person if they measure up to our standard. The only problem with that is nobody will ever measure up. *We have to be loyal because it is a characteristic of God, not because people are perfect.* I'm not saying you don't have standards or that you follow people blindly. You must hear from the Lord to know you are in the right place. There is a process to correctly communicate if things are mishandled, but if God has placed you under a particular leader and spoken to you clearly that this is where you are to serve, then serve with a loyal heart! You can't just leave every time you have a conflict or issues arise. People who leave at the first sign of conflict become like "spiritual gypsies" bouncing around from church to church.

God's plan is for you to work through your difficulties. It's part of the growth process.

If you are around a person for any length of time, you will see their flaws. People who are under me can see my flaws. I'm not perfect. Neither is any leader. *If you leave a leader just because you can see his flaws, then one day people will leave you as soon as they notice yours.* This is the biblical principle of reaping what you sow. There are times when I'll have strong convictions about something that are different from the leader that I'm called to serve. I'm not talking about sin issues or morality issues, but different convictions about the way ministry should be done or about the way things are carried out. Still, I am called to submit to my leader and be loyal to what God has put in their heart. And it is *okay* if there are different viewpoints. This is normal. Loyalty, however, requires us to honor and respect authority through the demonstration of forbearance, patience, and self-control.

Whenever something negative happens to you, you have the choice to be loyal to God or to let bitterness into your heart. You must bring that situation to the Lord. If Joseph hadn't come to the Lord, he would have hated his brothers forever. You have to be careful not to let negative events create lies in your life. In those times, you have to be careful not to listen to the wrong voice, but draw near to God and let Him speak truth to you. If you begin to believe lies, you will build up a defense in your heart. You will become defensive and calculated about everything. You may even come to the place where you're not willing to be vulnerable anymore.

Culture of Rebellion

In the 1960s, the Chinese Cultural Revolution had this effect on many people. The younger generation came against their parents, and as a result, the whole society was turned upside down. There was so much hurt and pain that people became afraid to be vulnerable with one another. Today there is a saying in China that if you develop a relationship with someone, you should only share 30 percent of your heart and keep the other 70 percent hidden. They are afraid to be open and vulnerable. To be closed and protected has become the default in Chinese culture. Furthermore, Chairman Mao, the Chinese communist revolutionary, told the people, "There is no such thing as love without an ulterior motive." When people in China believe this lie, then they suspect that even a friend's best intention has the worst motive. It has taken me more than twenty years to earn the people's trust in China. Lies and defenses can be individual or they can be cultural. Either way, in order to heal, we must be willing to trust and be a part of the body of Christ.

People who are wounded and defensive can become like porcupines. They go around with their quills sticking out, poking others. Have you ever been poked by a porcupine? It hurts! It also festers and creates a tender wound until healed. When this happens, people who have been poked recoil to protect themselves. It's a natural response. But something else happens too. When a porcupine sticks someone and is rejected by them, it reinforces the original lie they believed which causes them to become even more hardened. These people become hyper-sensitive and others feel like they are walking on eggshells around them. But here's the deal. A dead man cannot be sensitive! Galatians 2:20 reads, *"I have been crucified with Christ and I no longer live, but Christ lives in me. The life I now live in the body, I live by faith in the Son of God, who loved me and gave Himself for me"* (NIV).

If you die with Christ, you can live with Christ! Just because a leader hurt you in the past, doesn't mean you can't trust any leader at all. Exposing the lie and believing the truth disarms this vicious cycle. You cannot control other people or events that may take place, but you can control your reaction. Whether you will believe the lie or become defensive is up to you.

When I went through the difficult situations that I shared with you in the previous chapter, I could have believed the lie that all pastors will mistreat me. Instead, I asked God to search my heart and make me more like Jesus. Because when we die to ourselves, we let Christ live through us. It becomes about

His power, the Holy Spirit working in us, instead of us reacting in the flesh. And when we talk about loyalty, this has to be a part of the conversation. We need to address hurts in our lives. Otherwise, our festering wounds will affect our ability to be in healthy relationships with others. We will become porcupines ourselves, inflicting wounds. It will also affect our ability to be *loyal*. The enemy is working hard to get us to focus on negative situations or people who have offended us, rather than lifting our eyes up to Him. If you allow God to heal the hurts in your life, you will be able to experience the anointing that comes from walking in God's ways.

The Pursuit of Loyalty

There are many men and women throughout the Bible who chose to live before God and people with a loyal heart. Second Kings tells the story of how Elisha followed Elijah. He pursued him and stayed loyal to him. Elisha followed Elijah from Gilgal to Bethel. Elijah told him to stay there, but Elisha was loyal and followed him into Jericho. Again, Elijah told him to stay there, but in his loyalty, Elisha followed Elijah across the Jordan. Each time he said to his leader, *"If you are going, I am going with you."* It was in Elisha's heart to follow Elijah right up until God took him away in a whirlwind. Elisha was loyal to the end, and because of his loyalty, he received a double portion of Elijah's anointing.

Ruth also demonstrated a loyal heart. In Ruth 1:16, Ruth told Naomi, *"Don't ask me to leave you and turn back. Wherever you go, I will go; wherever you live, I will live. Your people will be my people, and your God will be my God"* (NLT). She was loyal. My wife, Ruth, has been loyal to me like Ruth was to Naomi. God gave me this revelation as I was thinking about how much my wife has done for me through the years, how she has followed me, ministering all over the world. Even though I am a US citizen, I am Chinese by birth. Ruth, however, is fully American. Yet we have lived and ministered in China for more than two decades and she has said that my people are her people! Wow. Try and wrap your mind around her faithfulness. In this day and age, that is truly remarkable. Wherever I go, she will go! God also showed me that because Ruth chose to be loyal, she received a supernatural peace and joy in the midst of life's various circumstances. I am so thankful that God blessed me with such an amazing wife!

Aaron and Hur are another great example of loyalty. They were loyal to Moses, holding his hands up while Joshua led the army in battle. Joshua made a declaration of loyalty when he emphatically stood before the people and said, *"As for me and my house, we will serve the Lord!"* (Joshua 24:15). David was loyal too, even when Saul tried to kill him. But because he had a loyal heart, David attracted 400 mighty warriors that were loyal to him. They were able to be changed from disillusioned and distressed men into loyal followers, all because

David had a loyal heart (1 Samuel 22:2). If you've had a bad leader, like Saul was to David, you can still honor God just like David did. Loyalty breeds loyalty and David was blessed with loyal men under him.

The example of Korah in Numbers 16, on the other hand, shows what happens to a rebellious leader who is disloyal. Korah formed a power-grabbing scheme and came against the leadership of Moses and Aaron. It wasn't enough for him to be disloyal himself, but he rallied other leaders to also stand against them. However, Moses and Aaron didn't fight with the flesh. Instead, Moses immediately called on the Lord. This story speaks to me because my *old self* would fight with my own flesh. If I hadn't let God change me and someone like Korah had come against me, I would have fired back in self-righteousness. Now, my desire is to be like Moses and turn to God. Moses and Aaron said, *"Let's let God prove who is right and who is wrong!"* Long story short, Korah along with his rebellious followers, including their families, died. More than 14,000 people were swallowed by the earth. They were disloyal, but vengeance belonged to God who brought punishment on disloyal hearts.

Perhaps it is difficult to imagine the catastrophic effects of the previous biblical scene, but we have a modern-day example that can help us imagine it. In 2008, in the northwest of Chengdu, China, the Wenchuan earthquake, with a magnitude of 8.0, caused more than 68,000 people to lose their lives in a matter of minutes. Several weeks after the quake, I traveled with a humanitarian team to the area in a van filled with much needed supplies. While we were up in a remote mountain village, we noticed a massive mound of dirt that was located in an unnatural place. After asking around, some of the locals explained that a group of officials had come in a motorcade to celebrate the opening of a new resort hotel. As they were conducting the ribbon cutting ceremony, the earthquake struck, sending the officials and their vehicles up into the air. The earth pulled apart and everything came down into the chasm. As the earthquake continued, the earth pushed together again and swallowed everybody and everything. Tragically, the entire gathering of people, vehicles and all, were buried alive.

Loyalty vs. Disloyalty

These biblical examples of people who were loyal or disloyal serve as prime examples to us. Personally, I am grateful for God teaching me that He will fight for me and I do not have to, nor should I, fight on my own behalf. When we walk in the *Spirit* instead of the *flesh*, God will bring justice and take care of every situation we face. By His power, not our own, we can remain loyal to Him.

In my lifetime, I've had many experiences with the principle of loyalty, both with leaders over me and with leaders under me. Loyalty is something God wants you to encounter personally. He will give you opportunities and you will be tested in your loyalty. But you can't even begin to imagine how much God can use you if you grab onto this truth! If you have been hurt, let God heal you. Turn every situation over to Him and allow Him to work in your heart. He will turn those negative situations into triumphs as you refuse to believe a lie. God will then take you to another elevation!

It is my prayer that we begin to see and experience the spirit of loyalty before we receive its *definition*. I don't want the concept of loyalty to be merely head knowledge, but rather something that is interwoven into the fabric of our hearts. It becomes part of who we are, living a life that is always loyal to God and His Kingdom, His righteousness, His leadership, and His church. Loyalty is solidarity. It is a sense of belonging that comes with wholeheartedness. Further, loyalty is fidelity, faithfulness, reliability, and dependability, galvanized with unswerving devotion. We submit to our local church leadership because our hearts are set on being loyal to God. In doing so, we can trust Him if leadership or our local church hurts us or mistreats us. Vengeance is God's and He will protect us and redeem any situation we face. *Let the spirit of loyalty come upon you today.*

Why are we loyal? We are not loyal out of fear. We don't walk with loyal hearts because we are anxious about what may happen if we don't. Unfortunately, some leaders preach fear of consequences to force capitulation. These types of leaders can be controlling and manipulative. Yet, the reason *why* we are loyal is simple. We are loyal because of relationship—our relationship with God. When we are in healthy, godly relationships, the response of our heart is loyalty. More abundant than the stories of disloyal people reaping the consequences are the many stories about people who served with a loyal heart because of their love for God and their leaders. Love and relationship are the fuel for godly loyalty that strengthens ministry everywhere they're found. And the local church is God's design for how He will move and build His Kingdom on earth. Jesus declared:

> "*This is the rock on which I will put together my church,*
> *a church so expansive with energy that not even the gates*
> *of hell will be able to keep it out. And that's not all. You*
> *will have complete and free access to God's kingdom, keys to*
> *open any and every door: no more barriers between heaven*
> *and earth, earth and heaven. A yes on earth is yes in heaven.*
> *A no on earth is no in heaven*" (Matthew 16:18-19 MSG).

When we are in wholehearted relationships based on God's love, we will find the right soil for loyalty to grow. The biblical concept of loyalty is purely relational. The core of the reason *why* we are loyal is because *God is loyal* and God is relational. Loyalty is a fruit of God's character in our lives. He is the foundation of loyalty, and He was loyal to us before we were loyal to Him. God was loyal to Moses and faithfully helped him lead the children of Israel. God was loyal to Abraham, keeping His promise and allowing Abraham and Sarah to have a son in their old age. God was loyal to Jacob even when Jacob acted deceitfully. God was loyal to David, even after he committed adultery and murder. God was loyal to Peter, and Paul, and Timothy, and the list goes on and on! God is a loyal God! He is a covenant God, and in His covenant, He is loyal for all of eternity. We love others because God loved us. We are loyal to God and loyal to those He has placed us in relationship with because He is loyal—this is our *why*.

Loyalty in Action

The story of Jonathan and his armor bearer, in 1 Samuel 14, is one of my favorite examples of a loyal heart. Jonathan wanted to attack the Philistine garrison, and his armor bearer responded with a perfect heart of loyalty in verse 7: *"So his armor bearer said to him, 'Do all that is in your heart. Go then; here I am with you, according to your heart.'"* This is loyalty! Jonathan's armor bearer had a relationship with Jonathan that was so strong, he didn't just follow him into easy situations, but he followed him into a battle where they were outnumbered. He was committed to his leader and fought by his side to the death. God gave them the victory and the two of them took the entire garrison! One day, when I was reading this story, it struck me that this was a picture of me in Estonia.

When in Estonia, I was loyal to Pastor Rei. I told him to do whatever was in his heart and I would stand with him. I didn't pursue the things God had put in my heart for the future, but supported the vision God had given Pastor Rei. I had come with a desire to build a New Testament church, but Pastor Rei was in an older, more traditional church. I told him I could help him build a New Testament church, but he told me he wanted to be faithful to do what God had called him to with the *traditional* church. By serving him with a loyal heart, God was preparing me for everything I would one day do in China. If I hadn't served with a loyal heart, I would not be serving in China the way I am today.

Sent versus Going

There is a difference between being "sent" and "going." It's critical and can be the difference between long-term effectiveness and anointing and a short-term flame-out. The heart check is this—if I am loyal to my local church leadership, it's better to be "sent" with their blessing and covering. This often requires patience on our part along with trusting that

God is in control, has a preferred method through which He works, and has perfect timing. Many times, when a person is impatient or bitter because of an offense, they choose to "go" on their own and be a missionary. Going is not biblical. The Bible never talks about you deciding to "go." It always talks about being "sent." Paul and Barnabas are a prime example. Acts 13:2-3 says, *"As they ministered to the Lord and fasted, the Holy Spirit said, 'Now separate to Me Barnabas and Saul for the work to which I have called them.' Then, having fasted and prayed, and laid hands on them, they sent them away."*

God called Ruth and me in 1981 to go to the foreign mission field. Our pastor at the time said they didn't have that mission, only local. We submitted to leadership and remained patient doing local missionary outreaches. Then, after a number of years, we were "sent." So, what does that tell you? Even when you are called to go, there is always a timing issue. Many people just go because they are impatient or offended and miss God's timing to be sent.

The things you are doing now are preparing you for the things God has for your future. You may not serve under a leader who has your vision, but it is possible that God put you there to teach you to obey authority, and to prepare you, while building your character. When you are loyal to the people God has called you to serve, you are reflecting God's character of loyalty, and moving closer to the fulfillment of God's calling on your life. Loyalty breeds loyalty.

I have ministered all over the world and have heard many people say that they can be loyal to God, but not to another human. Because of the misuse of authority, they have been wounded and hurt by leadership, or have been under someone who is controlling or manipulative. However, if you don't deal with your wounds, you will have a hard time being loyal, because loyalty is an issue of the heart. Ruth and I have walked through many situations where we have been mistreated, but we've learned to allow the Holy Spirit into those places, and you can too!

Questions for Reflection

1. What does the Bible have to say about being loyal?

2. Has your loyalty ever been tested through a negative experience?

3. When others are disloyal, do you still remain loyal to God and God's designated leaders?

4. When you read, "Loyalty breeds loyalty," how did that make you feel?

5. In what ways would you like to grow in loyalty in your life and ministry?

8

HEART OF
FAITHFULNESS

"And I thank Christ Jesus our Lord who has enabled me, because He counted me faithful."

—1 Timothy 1:12

The year was 1983 and more than ever, I was committed to my American dream of climbing the corporate ladder. As my favor at work increased, so did my self-confidence. I felt like no matter what I did, I would succeed. Not only did I feel successful at work, I felt like I would also be successful and influential in the local church that Ruth and I had recently joined. The thought never crossed my mind that I wouldn't flourish in anything I put my mind to.

I took pride in the fact that I was considered the guy you could count on, a man of his word, a man committed to growing the local church, and who could get the job done. Little did I know, God had much to teach me about what growing the local church really meant and more importantly what *faithfulness* meant. As a fourth-generation believer from Hudson Taylor's ministry, I had a great spiritual heritage, yet I had no idea how much God still needed to teach me.

Grateful to God for changing my life and blessing me in so many ways, I experienced an abundant amount of joy in worship. During worship, I would sing and praise with all my heart. God meant so much to me. Ruth and I had not attended this church for long, but we appreciated the sincere worship each Sunday. They had a wonderful praise and worship team, and my heart always felt full to overflowing as I freely sang out my love for Jesus each week.

Not many people know this, but along with singing, I also love to play the guitar. Well, one day I thought to myself, *"I love worship so much, I want to be on the worship team where I can sing on stage and inspire others to worship freely like I do."* I was so eager to serve God, and although I had only been at that church for a short time, I decided to ask the pastor if I could join the worship team. Wanting to serve in my church in any way I could, I was eager to build God's Kingdom. As a musician, I thought being on the worship team would be a great opportunity, and I wanted to make myself available for anything the pastor needed . . . or so I thought.

Thankfully, my pastor had a lot of wisdom. He could see that although I was sincere about wanting to serve, there was a part of me that liked the glamorous idea of being in front of the congregation with my guitar. My pastor said, "Well, we don't need any more people on our worship team right now, but we do need you." I felt excited inside, as I thought, *"Wow, they need me! I wonder what great ministry opportunity I will get to experience?"* My heart quickened a bit as I anticipated what he might ask me to do. *Whatever it was, I was ready!*

My pastor looked at me quietly as my enthusiasm continued to mount, and he explained that there was definitely an important job he needed done on a regular basis that would really serve the church. He continued, "Along with our Sunday services, we have leadership classes every weekend, and we are desperately in need of someone who would volunteer to come and clean the bathrooms every Saturday." He looked at me expectantly, as my heart dropped. I just stood there in silence, completely stunned. *What?!* I thought. *I am a business professional! I spend the week in my nice office, talking to important people, and helping to broker important deals, and you want me to come in on Saturday and clean toilets?!* Although I was thinking this, what came out of my mouth was, "I'll pray about it." This is what we Christians often say when we don't want to tell someone *no* right away. I was upset by his request and surprised by my internal reaction to the idea of being the weekend janitor.

My pride was still stinging with embarrassment by the time I arrived home, and I had made up my mind—*this is not my church*. I could not believe this man, who *used* to be my pastor, would ask me to clean toilets when I knew I had so much talent to offer. As I continued to fume and ponder how this church would be sorry to lose such a devoted and gifted member like me, the Holy Spirit began to speak. He began to reveal how I wasn't sincere in my request to serve the church. I was really looking for a position—a place of recognition and prestige. In that moment, the sweet counsel of the Holy Spirit ministered to me, and I was convicted of my attitude and pride. God was working in me, and I repented. I knew that I had to obey the voice of the Holy Spirit, even though my flesh was still wrestling with my wounded pride.

A few days later, I went to my pastor and told him I was willing to come and clean the toilets. Nothing in me wanted to do this job, and it wasn't a position I was bragging about or hoping someone would see me performing, but I wanted to say yes to God. Reluctantly, I arrived every Saturday to clean the bathrooms. I remember grabbing my mop and cleaning supplies and slowly making my way down the dark, empty corridor to the bathrooms. My heart was like a brick of disappointment in my chest as I scrubbed and polished the toilets. There were no stages, lights, microphones, or people watching, just the toilets and me.

While I was faithfully serving and doing my job each Saturday, my heart wasn't in it. I felt like I was so much better than this job. I had so much potential that was being wasted. Each time I entered the church on Saturday, it was as if my feet had suddenly gained a hundred pounds and I could hardly walk. My body felt stiff and my hands were tired before I had even started. Each week I forced myself to go, all the while wondering how an educated, successful man like me could be put in such a lowly and demoralizing position—cleaning toilets. While giving myself pep talks that I was okay, I had no idea that God was using this as a lesson to teach me faithfulness.

One Sunday morning, as Ruth and I sat down after worship, I couldn't help feeling like I should be up there on the stage leading the people. With my shoulders hunched forward, I grabbed my Bible and began looking for the passage of Scripture that our pastor told us to turn to. It was Colossians 3:23, and although I had read this Scripture many times, this was the day that it would brand its truth on my mind, forever changing me. The pastor's voice rose clearly as he said, *"Whatever you do, you are to do it with all your heart. When we are faithful in the little things and do them joyfully, it is like worship to the Lord."* As his words hung in the air, I was jolted by the realization that even though I was cleaning every Saturday, I wasn't doing it with a joyful heart, as worship unto the Lord. I realized I had been cleaning the bathrooms with the wrong attitude, dragging my feet as I grudgingly and half-heartedly worked. In that moment, the Holy Spirit convicted me and I repented immediately. If scrubbing the toilets could be as worship to the Lord then that was what I wanted. My heart's cry became *"God change me! Help me to do everything with a joyful heart, as worship to You."*

The next Saturday, with a new attitude, I cleaned the best I could and worked with all my heart as worship to the Lord. Then, right there, while I was cleaning toilets, the Holy Spirit came upon me! My mop became like my guitar! I was singing and dancing as joy filled my heart. From that day forward, I had such joy in cleaning those bathrooms. I saw my need to die to my flesh, and realized mopping the floors was a sacrifice of praise. God used this seemingly little experience to teach me about faithfulness.

Zechariah 4:10 reads, *"Do not despise these small beginnings, for the Lord rejoices to see the work begin, to see the plumb line in Zerubbabel's hand"* (NLT). God uses the seemingly little things as a plumb line to measure our faithfulness. In the same way, God will use the little things in our lives to train and prepare us for the greater things He has planned. Jeremiah 29:11 confirms this truth, *"'For I know the plans I have for you,' says the Lord. 'They are plans for good and not for disaster, to give you a future and a hope'"* (NLT). My ministry started in 1983 by cleaning the men's room and I know God rejoiced to see the work begin!

Faithful in the Small Things

The tiny little things we do when no one is looking will determine our level of faithfulness. When you have mundane tasks set before you, do them with joy, as worship to the Lord. God may unexpectedly bring a task your way that you don't like; however, it doesn't matter how little or mundane it is, or how much effort is required, what matters is that you do it with all your heart. So, let me ask you a few questions. How do you do the little things God gives you? How trustworthy are you with mundane tasks? When God entrusts you with a job or responsibility, do you finish it? Remember, when you serve with a faithful heart you are worshiping God, and He notices.

This lesson has never left me, and God began to expand my ministry after I learned it. As I served faithfully, my leaders noticed and asked me to participate in other ministry opportunities. Many years later, after we had moved away and been in ministry quite a while, the leaders from my old church were attending a large conference. The conference was in the same city as my old church. Unbeknownst to them, I was one of the speakers. I hadn't seen them in more than two decades, and as they were sitting there, I came up and preached about the Father's love. There were a few thousand people in attendance, and the leaders of my old church couldn't believe it when they saw me. They couldn't believe that this Chinese man who used to be at their church could be serving in this capacity. The current pastor of the church was just a small boy when I attended and cleaned toilets. After seeing me preach at this conference, the new pastor invited me to come back to my old church to preach.

On Saturday, the day before I spoke, the Holy Spirit quickened my heart to ask the pastor to take me to the church early in the morning. When we arrived, I walked right into the men's room. I opened the door and stood there in front of the toilets I used to clean. Everything looked the same as I vividly recalled wrestling with the Lord and encountering the Holy Spirit while struggling to clean. Standing there, I began to weep. I was so thankful for the sweet conviction of the Holy Spirit. Had God not moved on me and had I not surrendered to Him during that time in my life, I would have never reached my destiny. I would have never experienced all that God had for me.

The pastor asked, "Are you alright?" He had no idea of all God had done in my life since the time when I was there.

He had no idea how God taught me to be faithful in the little things and to give a sacrifice of praise to the Lord in all I did. Since that time when I served as a janitor, God has taken me all over the world to minister in multiple countries. You see, our ministry to the Lord and to others starts when we are faithful in the little things. The character of God is faithful. And when we are faithful, we are reflecting the character of God. It brings God glory when we are faithful in the small things. *God gives us the choice and we have to decide if we will be faithful.* Our choice then determines our destination. It is my desire that God would raise up more people that are faithful in the little things.

Stewardship

Not only is faithfulness reflected in how we complete the small tasks God gives to us, it is also reflected in our stewardship. Stewardship simply means the way we manage or care for that which God has given us. It is wise to evaluate yourself and ask God if you are a good steward. When we faithfully manage someone else's things, God can trust us with more. When we are faithful, we are good stewards. In Matthew 25, Jesus tells the parable of the talents. In this story, the stewards that were faithful with the small things were rewarded and received more. Whatever God has given you to do, do it with all your heart. Good leaders demonstrate faithfulness toward responsibility and commitment. Wherever God puts you, make sure you are faithful. You are not just fulfilling an obligation. You are serving the Lord. Ephesians 6:6-8 reads, *"As slaves of Christ, do the will of God with all your heart. Work with enthusiasm, as though you were working for the Lord rather than for people. Remember that the Lord will reward each one of us for the good we do, whether we are slaves or free"* (NLT). I have seen many people in my life that are extremely gifted, but they are not faithful. I would rather have one faithful person on my team than twenty gifted people.

Being faithful is synonymous with being a good steward. Luke 16:10-12 states: *"He who is faithful in a very little thing is faithful also in much; and he who is unrighteous in a very little thing is unrighteous also in much. Therefore if you have not been faithful in the use of unrighteous wealth, who will entrust the true riches to you? And if you have not been faithful in the use of that which is another's, who will give you that which is your own?"* (NASB). When we are faithful, we manage the property of others well and it is a reflection of our hearts. God will use little things in your life to train you to be faithful. He will also test you to see how faithful you are when no one is looking. When you are faithful with the things that belong to someone else, you don't have to be constantly reminded of your commitments. A faithful person can be trusted to do the task, no matter what.

Can I Borrow Your Boat?

Early in His ministry, Jesus was walking by the seashore and had need of a boat. The Bible says, *"Then He got into one of the boats, which was Simon's, and asked him to put out a little from the land. And He sat down and taught the multitudes from the boat"* (Luke 5:3). When Jesus was finished teaching, He told Simon to launch the boat into the deep and let down his nets for a catch. When they obeyed again, they couldn't contain all the fish!

Years before he became a great leader of the church, Simon Peter obeyed Jesus by simply letting Him borrow his boat. Sometimes, actually quite often, before God can use us for the "bigger" things, He asks to borrow our boats. Our boat could be taking time to set up chairs or sound systems. It could be bringing lunch to our leaders or cleaning and selling bottles in Estonia. It could even be cleaning bathrooms. One thing is for certain, before we launch out in the deep for a big catch, Jesus is going to ask to borrow your boat.

Hudson Taylor's Legacy

But what is faithfulness? Faithfulness means that we consistently keep our trust and focus on God. If we take care of God's business, He will take care of ours. When I think about Hudson Taylor, I think about a man who demonstrated faithfulness and who consistently focused on God. He served

God faithfully in China, and here I am four generations later. I am so grateful that he was faithful.

Hudson Taylor was born in Barnsley, England, in 1832. Today, however, there is no monument to commemorate his success. Yet, because he served faithfully as a missionary in China, hundreds of Chinese tourists go to Barnsley each year. The modern-day citizens of Barnsley had never heard of Hudson Taylor, but after many, many Chinese people kept coming, the mayor realized he needed to discover who Hudson Taylor was and why numerous Chinese people continued to visit his town. Instead of building a monument for himself, Hudson Taylor built God's Kingdom. *He was faithful and now his legacy lives on in my heart and in the hearts of the Chinese people.* Hudson Taylor was a *Puren*.

Not only was Hudson Taylor faithful, he also taught other men and women to be faithful. He raised leaders in successive generations, and these men and women then taught others. The legacy of Hudson Taylor's faithfulness continues to this day because he built for *permanence*. Hudson Taylor modeled his leadership after Paul the Apostle. Paul was not just faithful himself, but he raised other faithful men who would also teach and train others after them.

In 1 Timothy 1:12, Paul writes that God counted him faithful and therefore placed him into ministry. He was the first generation and then passed his faithfulness onto his spiritual son, Timothy. I know that if I'm ever going to build faithful men, I must be faithful. We can only reproduce what we are. If you desire to raise up other leaders, you first must be faithful. Above all, you must be faithful to Christ, letting Him lead you. I have been on the mission field for more than thirty years, including my years in Estonia. Because of following God's leading in my life, I now have more joy, more zeal, and more passion than ever. Just as Paul passed the baton to Timothy, I am intentional about passing the baton to the men and women God has entrusted to me. You can be too, but you must first obey God and steward what He gives you.

Building for Permanence

In the same way that Timothy was faithful like Paul, we read in 2 Timothy 2:2 an instruction Paul gave him to find and train other faithful men and women so they too could teach others. Timothy trained faithful men, and those men passed his DNA on to others. This biblical pattern reveals the impact of faithfulness. Jesus, the ultimate example of faithfulness, poured into twelve disciples. Those disciples faithfully trained others, and today, as we follow the biblical pattern, we will build for permanence.

The more you show yourself faithful and steward well the things God entrusts you with, the more He will give you. God will give you what belongs to Him when He finds you trustworthy. And you'll know that your heart is in the right place when you understand that everything you receive is God's and you steward it well. Use every opportunity to develop faithfulness in your life. Be faithful with whatever God has given you today. Be faithful with the small tasks and serve your leaders with a faithful spirit.

In 1 Samuel 16, the Bible tells us that David was a faithful shepherd. He was on the backside of the hills with the sheep when God told the prophet Samuel to anoint David as king. This shows how God will put you into ministry based on faithfulness, not man's praise. The Bible is clear that God exalts the humble but resists the proud. David was called to be king, and while he was being faithful tending sheep and ministering to King Saul, God was preparing him for something greater. Wherever God has you right now, be faithful. Focus on doing the best where you are. Even if you aren't promoted, that's okay! You are doing it for God.

Many leaders fall because of a lack of faithfulness. They didn't learn its principle before their promotion, and I've seen the unfortunate consequences. They have a lack of faithfulness to their spouse, to God's Kingdom finances, even to glorify God. Faithfulness is being trustworthy. Even if it is difficult, embrace every opportunity God gives you to learn faithfulness. These difficult times can be valuable lessons. *"Dear brothers and sisters, when troubles of any kind come your way, consider it an opportunity for great joy. For you know that when your faith is tested, your endurance has a chance to grow. So let it grow, for when your endurance is fully developed, you will be perfect and complete, needing nothing"* (James 1:2-4 NLT).

Gobi Desert

In my life, I have had to learn to be faithful in the most mundane tasks, like the story of cleaning the toilets. But through my actions, God has seen the faithfulness of my heart and He has entrusted me with more. I remember the time I was in a remote place in the Gobi Desert. I was training fifty house leaders and we were doing a lock-in for five days. We would stay there, sleep there, eat there, and spend ten-hours a day in training. These leaders were hungry for God! We had to find a discreet place where we could spend time together without interference from the outside. We didn't bring cell phones or anything else that might give away our location or be a distraction. We were there to focus on God, and I wanted these leaders to have the training they needed to lead their house churches.

I was faithfully serving in China where my name was unknown to the outside world. I wasn't looking to promote myself in any way but to simply serve leaders faithfully. While we were there, I received a message through a third party that

I had a call from an influential pastor in America. Since we didn't have phones with us, someone had to bring me a phone so I could talk to him during a break. Another leader in China had let him know about the ministry I had been faithful with for years. This influential pastor told me he was bringing together key leaders from different regions of the world, and he wanted me to be a part of that team. He offered to fly Ruth and me to the United States. After we met with him, he invited us to be a part of his team over an area of Asia.

As I served faithfully in obscurity, God saw the work, and in His timing allowed me to have a much greater influence with key leaders around the world. If I hadn't been faithful in the small things, I would have never been given this opportunity. When you are faithful, you never have to make your name known or strive for acknowledgment. God will promote you as He did with King David. When you are trustworthy with what is important to God, you have unlimited potential, and God will entrust you with greater resources, talents, and giftings.

Be Faithful

When we build for faithfulness and permanence, we are not looking for the quick fix, and we are not building for appearances or man's approval. *Building for permanence instead of appearance is what makes the difference on whether or not you will last in ministry.* When you build a house, you don't want someone to come in and do a rush job. Rather, you want someone who will take his or her time and build with precision so the house is strong. If we do this with our own houses, we should certainly do this with God's house! Building for permanence is something we are committed to for the long term. It is a relational covenant of trust and commitment. God may change the circumstances between you and the person, but your mentality should be to build for permanence and for the success of others. This type of relationship will look different with different people, but the goal is to be faithful. If you are faithful to those you are serving, through your example, they will be able to better raise up others. Wherever you are, be faithful! No matter how mundane the task, be faithful! If you want to reach your full destiny in God, be faithful!

Questions for Reflection

1. Have you ever had to do a menial task in ministry?

2. How could those menial tasks be a part of God's preparation for your ultimate call?

3. In which areas in your life is God asking you to be faithful, even when it feels distasteful, menial, or mundane?

4. Do you view the things you do right now as having a lasting impact for His Kingdom?

5. How trustworthy are you with mundane tasks?

6. When God entrusts you with a job or responsibility, do you finish it with joy?

9

SERVING THROUGH
A BETRAYAL

*"My companion . . . violated his covenant. His speech was
smooth as butter, yet war was in his heart; his words were
softer than oil, yet they were drawn swords."*

—Psalm 55:20-21 ESV

Tears ran down my cheeks as I silently wept. It was
February 2004, and the movie *The Passion of the Christ* was
released. I felt drawn to see the movie repeatedly, and each
time as I watched the scene of Jesus in the garden of Gethsemane being betrayed by Judas, I shook inside as I wept for
Jesus. I didn't know at the time that God was preparing me
for my own betrayal from the kiss of a friend that would send
me running from the police.

When you serve God as a *Puren*, it doesn't matter what happens to you, you will remain faithful. Even if people betray you or treat you unfairly, you will serve Christ because of a pure heart, not because it is easy. When I was in China in 2004, there was a man I was training to take my place. I met him in 1999 when he was in the bottom of the pit. He had lost everything and I had compassion on him. After taking him from the state he was in, I bought him new clothes, fed him, gave him a drink physically and spiritually. Ruth and I made sure his needs were met as I trained him in the truth of God's Word. I poured my life into him and did everything I could do to bless him. As I trained him, I recognized the leadership potential in his life and wanted to train him up to eventually continue the work of the ministry in China. There were times when he and his family were out of money and Ruth and I would help them financially. We were so committed to his success that we gave our word to keep helping his family financially so he could continue to serve in ministry. As our relationship grew, he became a spiritual son and friend to me. I would speak into his life so he could grow and become stronger in the things of God.

One day, as we were discussing his family, the topic of his son and his son's wife came up. He came from a culture where only the father worked, even if the children were adults and married. His son had this same perspective. The son and his wife were both of working age and in their twenties, but instead of working, they chose to live with the father so that he could completely support them. Not only did they not work, they also did nothing productive with their time. I was careful in giving any counsel, but since we were supporting his family financially and knew they were struggling, I wanted to talk with him about this situation. I was careful in how I communicated it to him, but didn't realize I had offended him. I had spent years with him and had his family's best interest in mind. After this conversation, rather than clearly letting me know he had a different perspective, he instead began to undermine Ruth and me, as well as slander our reputation to other people in our ministry network.

After some time had passed, I heard about some of the things he was saying and doing. I didn't know how I should respond. We were supporting him and his family every month. We had entrusted many things to him; yet, we kept hearing that he was speaking negatively about us. With a heavy heart, I talked with Ruth about what to do. As usual, she had God's wisdom and encouraged me that since I had committed to supporting him through the end of the year, I should keep my commitment to him financially.

I really wanted to talk with him and make things right. Finally, we were able to arrange a time to travel and meet with him and his wife. Before I met with him, I asked God to give me a father's heart for him. Although Ruth and I wanted to meet with them as a couple to talk, his wife didn't come. Though he had turned against me, I wanted to look past his offense and reconnect with him. I wanted to have a conversation like we used to have when I first found him and he was so eager to learn and grow in the things of God. Yet, when we sat down to talk, it was a very awkward conversation. His heart was not there and he had brushed me off. When I realized we couldn't connect and he didn't want to talk with me, I gave him the final monthly support money that I had committed to giving him. As I slid the envelope across the table to him, rather than the gracious, thankful way he used to respond to me, he took the money, stood up, and left without saying anything.

The next month, he made an announcement to everyone in the ministry network that he had cut off relationship with me. He had primarily been working with the leaders in one region of China, and when the leaders in that region heard about this, they tried to track me down to ask me what had happened. Although he was the primary leader, I had a good relationship with them, and they were concerned when they heard he was not working with me anymore. When they called me, I asked, "Well, what did you hear?" He had told them he had parted company because I had a doctrinal error. I asked what the doctrinal error was and they said, "Well, he didn't clarify, but he said he wanted all of us to sever our relationship with you." I said, "If I have a doctrinal error, I am willing to talk openly about it and receive correction if I'm wrong. Why don't you invite both of us to sit in front of all of you and the elders in the northern region and we can have a discussion? We can talk through any doctrinal issue together and you all can make a decision about what you think is correct. If I have made a doctrinal error that is truly wrong, then you can all leave and I'll respect your decision. But at least allow me to defend myself and talk about it together." I then told the leaders that the fact of the matter was that there were no doctrinal issues. The real reason he had parted company is that he had taken up an offense. This was not a doctrinal issue, but a relational issue.

Offenses

Many times, in church, people get offended. Rather than admitting what they are offended about, and talking through it, they sugarcoat it and say they have a doctrinal issue so they can just stand up and leave. In reality, however, most offenses are relational, not doctrinal. In Matthew 18, Jesus gives clear direction about the appropriate way to handle an offense. We are first to go to the person and talk openly and honestly. If there is an unrepentant heart, then bring in a second person to have the conversation. And if there is still no resolution, it is then brought before the church.

God's pattern of dealing with offense leads us to open, honest conversations that are meant to be relational. Blaming something on a doctrinal issue and not being willing to discuss it is not the right way to resolve a conflict. After this conversation, I took time to process the correct way to handle it and planned a trip to the north to speak face-to-face with the leaders and my friend who was bringing accusations. I was willing to work through any issues in a healthy, relational, and biblical way. Soon, I was able to arrange the trip, but unfortunately the man who had taken up offense was not willing to meet, and he never came.

While spending time with one of the house churches in the region, we heard a *warning* knock at the door. Knowing that the police wouldn't allow church meetings in homes, we knew this signal meant we had to get out as fast as possible. The church leaders and I got out just in time and fled to the next village. In China, the house churches regularly suffer persecution, so this was nothing new. This time, however, the police were relentless. They followed us from village to village late into the night. I remember being exhausted. Some Christians in one of the villages were kind enough to give us some hot soup. But just as we began eating our soup, the Christians gave us the signal that the police were coming again.

Already fatigued, we dropped our spoons and ran to our car. We could not use flashlights the whole night, as we were trying to escape. Our only light as we traveled was the light of the moon. Suddenly, as we were driving out of the village, the police came into the village and we passed each other. All of us except the driver ducked low in the car. Because it was so dark, the police didn't know it was our car and drove past us. It was a close call. Finally, we made it to a big city where it was a little easier to blend in. This was the city I was supposed to fly out of, so we found a safe place to stay the night. While it's normal for the police to interfere with Christians worshiping, we were wondering why the police relentlessly pursued us. As we discussed a strategy in the hotel, I thought perhaps I would leave my entire luggage there in the city. I reasoned that I could travel without any luggage making things easier, and I would simply pick it up the next time I was in the region.

Every time I travel to meet leaders, I bring things for teaching and encouraging them. This time I had a book I had written for our leaders to use and videotapes of me preaching. This material is extremely incriminating if I were to be captured by the police. We gathered all my videotapes and sensitive documents and we put them into some carry-on luggage. Then we decided it would be smart to travel separately from the bags, so we gave them to the pastor's younger sons to bring to me later in the day.

As the pastor's sons climbed into the taxi, the driver, seeing they were just kids with two bags, cheated them. He pretended the car wouldn't start and suggested they try to help push it to get it started. When they got out, he took off with the bags. All of the highly-sensitive material was in those bags: videos of me preaching, material for training leaders, and much of my other important teaching information. When I heard my bags had been stolen, I was deeply disappointed to have lost so many of my teaching resources. Also, the material in the wrong hands could be incriminating. But God was in control.

Since my carry-ons had been stolen, I arrived at the airport with only one small bag with my remaining things. At the airport, the police quickly identified and stopped me. They began searching through the one bag I had with me. They read all my papers with teaching material on them. Although it wasn't much, they obtained enough evidence to take me away in handcuffs. They also sent police to grab the couple that brought me to the airport. The other man I was traveling with was already on the plane and had called his wife to let her know he was coming home. The plane was taxiing out of the runway, but the police had the plane taxi back. They yanked him off the plane and arrested him too.

We were used to living in a communist country where freedom of religion is not allowed, but we had never experienced this type of pursuit. Later, I found out they had set up a sting operation in that airport. They had replaced some of the normal workers who would be at the airport with police officers. They did this to catch me! They had police at the train and bus stations as well. *Why all this effort just to catch me?* It broke my heart to later learn that all this was because of the man who was offended by me, the man I had helped when he was hungry, the one I took under my wing, the one I raised up to replace me someday as the overseer of this work. This very man reported to the police that I was an international cult leader. The police took this information seriously and they waited for me at the airport, the bus station, and the train station. They were determined to catch me. When they finally arrested me, they began shouting at me as I was handcuffed. I remember sitting there stunned, my hands cuffed behind my back as they screamed into my face, "We don't care where you're from! Even if you're from Mars, if you violate our laws, we will put you in jail!"

A few months earlier, the movie *The Passion of the Christ* had come out while we were in America. I remembered when I watched that movie for the first time and they were in the garden when Judas betrayed Jesus. In that moment, I was glued to the movie. When I saw that scene, I was so moved that I was weeping and crying. Ruth watched it with me, and she had no idea why I was crying so much over that scene. When the movie finished, it had touched such a deep place in my heart that I told Ruth I had to go back and see it a second time. I went back to the theater, and again I was so connected with that scene. I went back a third, fourth, and finally, a fifth time. I was the only person sitting in the matinee that last time, and I was right in the middle, all alone, weeping over that scene. Only God knew all I would be facing months later as the imagery of this scene was branded into my mind.

At the moment where I was sitting handcuffed on the floor, while they were shouting at me, humiliating me, and harassing me, the scene of Christ's betrayal played over and over in my mind. I visualized when Jesus was betrayed and the way He walked with such love and humility. He was quiet, and I knew I needed to imitate Christ. The police roughly hauled me to the detention center as if I were a POW, all the while trying to terrorize and intimidate me. Once at the cold, concrete compound, they used food and sleep deprivation tactics to wear me down. After they physically and mentally drained my energy reserves, a bright spotlight pierced my eyes as one officer after another shouted at me and grilled me with questions. Their relentless interrogation was intended to exhaust me to the point of collapse. But God is faithful, and He gave me strength in my thoughts as the scene from *The Passion of the Christ* kept replaying in my mind.

They stripped me down to nothing but a T-shirt and underwear. They had two guards on me, and they watched me even when I went to the bathroom. I couldn't even do that alone. I remember in the movie when Jesus prayed to his Father. As I sat in my cold cell, my every move being watched, that scene came to my mind. I asked them if I could just get down on my knees and pray. The guards knew I was a Christian, and for some reason they said I could pray. When I prayed, God comforted my heart. I knew if Jesus went through imprisonment for me, God would give me the strength to withstand imprisonment for Him.

Finally, the chief of police arrived and they brought me back to the interrogation room. After enduring more yelling and questioning, the chief eyed me with contempt and told me what a fool I was. Trying to trigger an angry reaction, the chief told me a former friend had turned me in. He told me the man had made a fool out of me. The chief of police began laughing at me and mocking me as he went on about how stupid I was. Knowing I had been educated in the west, he ridiculed me for giving money and support to a man who had then gone and turned me in. They tried to provoke me to anger so I would retaliate and speak against him out of revenge. They were pressing me; they wanted the names of other church leaders. I kept quiet, just as Jesus did when He was accused. I didn't say anything until he asked me one question. He asked, "Why did you do this? Why did you do so much for this guy who turned you in?" God put the answer in my heart as I calmly replied, "I did it because I love him." In that moment, the whole place became quiet. You could have heard a pin drop. None of them said anything after they heard the word *love*.

The guards shuffled me back to my cell. While I was being held, the Chinese Religious Bureau was checking all the materials I had with me at the airport. I imagined they were looking for any reason they could find to put me away for life, or send me to one of their labor camps in a remote city. They were evaluating the few teaching papers I had with me to see if they could prove I was an international cult leader. They only needed one doctrinal issue to convict me. After scouring the papers I had in my possession, they could find no doctrinal errors they could use to accuse me, and the religious bureau called the police chief and gave the order for my release.

On Good Friday, after being betrayed by someone I had called friend, I was taken to a detention center and treated like a criminal. But before they released me, one of the police assigned to me waited until no other police were around. When we were alone, he asked if I would pray for him. He wanted to become a Christian. After I prayed for him, he asked if I would pray for his father who had a chronic disease. He could only ask me this quietly when nobody else was around. He had watched me for seventy-two hours and saw my heart, and he saw that I had no desire to retaliate in response to the man who had betrayed me. This police officer was open to give his life to the Lord before I left the jail that day because he saw how I had love for a man who had treated me wrongly and I would not repay evil with evil. On Resurrection Sunday, this officer was about to be resurrected into everlasting life with Jesus. Finally, the door to my cell was opened, and I was free! I looked up to heaven and thanked God. I had been arrested three days ago on Friday— Good Friday. But they could only hold me for three days! On Resurrection Sunday, I was released!

If the police had caught me with the bags that were stolen by the taxi driver, my arrest could have turned out much differently. The religious bureau would have seen me preaching and teaching in the house church. As a foreigner, I am not allowed to proclaim Christ in that way and they would have taken me to jail! Or I could have been kept three years in the labor camps in the Gobi Desert. God is so good to have allowed my bags to be stolen!

Right after my arrest, Ruth and I were forced to leave China within nine days. We had no choice but to return to America. Upon our return, when we shared our story, everybody we met with told us not to go back to China. They told us we had done enough good work there in China and now we needed to stay put in America. I understood their hearts. They cared about us and our safety. But we knew we were called to serve God as under-rowers. We knew that our lives were meant to bring God glory, no matter the cost.

As Ruth and I were seeking God concerning His next step for us, we read in Acts where Paul was stoned after preaching and left for dead. After God touched Paul, he didn't retire to a life of safety. No, he went right back to Lystra, the very city where he had been stoned (Acts 14:19-20). After reading this, it confirmed to us that we needed to go back. We made our plans, and within thirty days we were on our way back to China.

Upon our return, we had decided to go in through two different borders just in case they arrested me, so it would not affect Ruth. We synchronized our watches, boarded our separate planes, and planned to call each other by 4:00 p.m. if everything was okay. When she arrived, she went through immigration and customs smoothly. With my new passport, I passed through immigration without a problem. But when it came to checking the luggage, I was pulled aside to another room. They went through all my things. I had no idea what was going on, and they wouldn't tell me what they were looking for. I wondered if I had walked right back into the lion's den. Quietly I prayed as they rummaged through my things. After a thorough search and lots of talking, they couldn't find what they were looking for and they let me enter the country. Five minutes before 4:00 p.m. I called my wife and said, "We're in!"

We returned to China for a visit and found the church growing and multiplying. Ruth and I have even returned to the city where the man lives who betrayed me and to the city where I was arrested. When we went back to that city, I went to where the detention center was, just to see it. Since I had been there, something had happened and it had been flattened into rubble. I stood upon the rubble, lifted my hands, and praised God! The Lord had vindicated me from this betrayal by removing the scars of my wounds. Betrayal is like someone stabbing you in the back with a knife when you are least prepared. I personally experienced betrayal and got a glimpse of what the Lord went through for our sins when He was betrayed.

I have given my life to be a servant of Christ, an under-rower. I know this life is not easy and we may face many trials, but as under-rowers, we are called and destined to take God's bride to her glory. It doesn't matter how people may treat you. We are to win souls and make disciples and serve without man's praise or recognition. There are people on the upper deck of the ship, the church, and what they are doing is their business. It's between them and God. As for you, God formed you in your mother's womb, and He has given you the honor of serving Him before you were even born.

Hold on to the call God has given you and serve faithfully as an under-rower, even when it is difficult, even if you are betrayed. *A life lived for God's glory, as an under-rower, is the highest calling of God!*

Questions for Reflection

1. What is your understanding of betrayal? Has this ever happened to you in your life?

2. If your answer is yes, how have you handled your betrayal? How have you gone through the cross like Jesus to win the victory?

3. Having gone through betrayal, have you learned to "distrust"? Or how have you learned to "trust" regardless of whether or not it may happen again?

10

LEARNING TO BE
A TRUE SON

"To Timothy, a beloved son. . . ."

—Paul[1]

My dad was the bravest man I've ever known, and I am proud to be his son. I knew what it meant to be a son in the natural, but I never knew what it meant to be God's son until I was twelve years old. Though I had attended church regularly, the things of God were not in my heart, nor was there a conviction of my need for Christ. I was a fourth-generation descendant of Hudson Taylor's ministry, but I had not received the heart of *sonship* from God.

---

[1] 2 Timothy 1:2

I remember like it was yesterday saying, "Mom! Why do I have to go to church? You go to church, but I don't want to! Give me five reasons why I should go!" Already, I was beginning to rebel against my parents. My two older sisters looked at me disapprovingly. They both liked going to church, and they attended Sunday school each week. While I was raised in a Christian home, I didn't want to believe in God just because my parents believed. And I didn't want to go to church just because my mom and dad told me to. While my mother understood the danger of my rebellious decision, she did give me a choice. Yet at the same time, she and the rest of the family put together a plan to lure me back to Christ. For several weeks after church at meal time, the family laughed, joked, and talked about all the wonderful relationships they had with the church community. They were very verbal about the joy they experienced in church. Since I had been absent for several weeks, I began to feel left out. I didn't want to miss the fun of belonging to a church community.

Our church had a big brother and big sister program where an older brother or sister in the Lord would get to know a young boy or girl to help them in their walk with the Lord. One of the big brothers felt like summer camp would be good for me, and he convinced me it would be fun. "I will be with you the whole time," he told me. "Anytime you have a need, I will help you." I was finally persuaded to go, but as soon as I arrived, the only thing I cared about was looking for girls! Here I was, twelve years old, sneaking out at night to smoke cigarettes with my friends, look for girls, and play pranks on the other boys at the camp. Connecting with God was the furthest thing from my mind.

But low and behold, on the third day, the preacher came and preached a powerful message about Christ's death on the cross. Tears began to flow down my cheeks as my heart was convicted of my need for Jesus. Until that moment, I never understood what it meant when God gave His only Son, Jesus, to die for my sins. I never understood how desperately I needed to receive the forgiveness that Jesus purchased for me at the cross, and I never knew how much I needed Jesus, how much I longed to be His *son*. It is hard to know what being a son or a child of God truly is, until you are one.

As the preacher was sharing his message, my heart began to beat faster and faster, and I knew that I needed God, not because my mom and dad knew God, not because my sisters knew God, but because I wanted to know God and receive His forgiveness personally. The moment came when the preacher invited any student to come up to the front if they wanted to give their lives to Christ, if they wanted to leave their sins at the foot of the cross. I fell to my knees and slowly began crawling to the front of the auditorium as tears streamed down my face. Unaware of the students on my left or my right, I was only aware of my desperate need for Jesus and to be God's son. As I bowed my head and prayed to God that He would forgive my sins and be Lord of my life, the Spirit of *sonship* came upon me (Romans 8:14-15). In that moment, I was birthed into God's Kingdom, and I have never looked back.

I remember this experience as though it were yesterday. Decades have passed since that day, but I still have the same Spirit of sonship upon my life. *This is important because we can never help others enter into the place of being spiritual sons and daughters until we have first experienced being the son or daughter of God.* We must first discover and experience what it is like when His love fills our hearts and overflows from inside of us. This is where all *"Puren"* sons and daughters begin—with the heart, through God's grace. Jesus is the Son of God; yet, He became the servant of God (Philippians 2:5-7). To be a *Puren* is to be a son that serves.

A Clinger, Not a Kisser

A *Puren* son is a clinger, not a kisser, because they have the same purpose as their Father and will do anything to serve Him. What do I mean by this? This metaphor is from the story of Naomi and Ruth. Naomi had two daughters-in-law. When Naomi decided to go back to her homeland of Judah, however, one of her daughters-in-law, Orpah, kissed her and left. Orpah decided to stay back and not travel with her to Judah. Ruth, on the other hand, clung to her and stayed faithful to her. *"But Ruth replied, 'Don't ask me to leave you and turn back. Wherever you go, I will go; wherever you live, I will live. Your people will be my people, and your God will be my God'"* (Ruth 1:16 NLT). Orpah was a kisser, but Ruth was a clinger.

A true servant in the faith is not a fair-weather friend, but he or she is committed for the long haul. They are not just a starter, but a finisher as well. Many people come to me and want to quickly connect with me. They call me all the relational terms, show affection, and have all the emotions, but they are nothing more than kissers. They want to get close to me so they can get what they want, and once they get whatever it is they want, they leave. Some who left me are the ones who later tried to destroy me. Some left quietly, but others, because of an offense, turned around and tried to devour me, discredit me, and destroy my ministry. Some of the sons I have loved the most have turned against me. I have learned that some people are just kissers, and that's not what I'm looking for. I'm looking for a clinger who has a sincere heart.

Every time I think of the story of Ruth, I think about my wife, Ruth. My beautiful wife is a clinger like Ruth (Now she is a good kisser too!). She clings to me the way Ruth clung to Naomi. She determined the day she married me that wherever I go, she will go; wherever I lodge, she will lodge; my country shall be her country; my people shall be her people; and my God shall be her God (Ruth 1:16). She rarely says anything to me with flowery words that don't have meaning. She is honest and stays right by my side. When I was arrested and put into jail, she could have easily done something to protect herself. But when she found out what had happened, she said to another pastor's wife that she was going to go to the city, track down where I was, and find out what happened to me. She had decided if she didn't hear from me within twenty-four hours, she was going to travel more than 1,200 miles straight to the Chinese police and plead with them to let me go. In our lives, we need more clingers, not kissers.

Another characteristic of a *Puren* son or daughter is that they are proven worthy, not a "Johnny-come-lately." *He will have loyalty and concern for his father's reputation.* No father is perfect, including me. I've made a lot of mistakes, and I will continue to make mistakes. But a true *Puren* servant will cover his father's shortcomings or embarrassments. I'm not talking about covering sin issues, but about covering mistakes or things that could cause shame.

Noah had three sons. After the ark had settled and Noah planted a vineyard, he became drunk and naked. One of the sons told the other two sons about his father not having any clothes on. When this happened, the other two covered their father. They would not expose their father's shame. They were proven worthy because they honored their father. Earlier, when I referenced Philippians 2:22 where Paul was talking about Timothy, he also says in that verse that Timothy had proven his worth. I've had a lot of *Puren* sons, but I've also had some hirelings. The hirelings have left me, but the *Puren* sons are still with me. If you've only had sons and daughters, when you find yourself with a hireling, it can be really difficult. You may treat them like sons and find out later they had bad motives. Sometimes they will try to get whatever they can out of you. *Puren* sons aren't looking to get anything out of me. They just believe I am a Kingdom man and they can see I love Jesus with passion. They also want to be Kingdom men and women and love Jesus with passion! A *Puren* servant connects with me and has pure motives, not selfish ambition or vainglory. They are proven worthy through their motives and actions over time.

A Faithful Envoy

Another attribute of a *Puren* son is that he is content with being his father's faithful envoy. In John 8:28, Jesus said He didn't do anything out of His own initiative, but He only said what the Father said and did what the Father did. Jesus was a faithful envoy for His Father. He was content in faithfully serving His Father. Similarly, in 1 Corinthians 4:17 Paul said, *"For this reason I have sent Timothy to you, who is my beloved and faithful son in the Lord, who will remind you of my ways in Christ, as I teach everywhere in every church."* Timothy was faithful, and he was an envoy for Paul, his spiritual father.

My *Puren* son is content to serve as my envoy. Just recently, we had many new believers come together in a city and they needed a shepherd. Many of them traveled hundreds of miles to hear me teach at a conference. After the conference, they asked me to send leaders to train them. They were sheep without a shepherd. I needed to evaluate the dynamics of the city and the environment there so I could send the right person to pastor them. It was important for me to have wisdom regarding which shepherd would be right for those sheep. Do you know who I sent? My *Puren* son! He was my envoy. I had complete trust that he knew my heart and understood my approach to ministry. I trusted his judgment and input. He took time to minister to the believers there, and after his return, he was able to give a thorough report on how the believers were doing. As a father in the faith, I know my true sons because they are content to be my envoy. I was able to travel and continue ministering in other cities because he went to that city on my behalf.

Pressing in for More

The next mark of a *Puren* son is that he is a pursuer. He presses in and draws life from his father. A true son does not need his father running after him to impart wisdom and counsel. He is wise enough to realize that his father has accumulated a deep wisdom over the years so he pursues him. In the same way that Elisha ran after Elijah, when a *Puren* son is with his father, he goes after him and pursues him to learn and glean. *Learning from a spiritual father is caught, not taught.*

A *Puren* son honors and respects his father, but he doesn't idolize him. There is a difference. Quite often in ministry, I've seen sons and daughters that are in awe of a spiritual father's revelation and teaching. Instead of merely respecting him, they place him on a pedestal. This is dangerous because the moment they discover he has a fault they are devastated, and in some cases, it ruins their fantasy. We should never idolize anyone. God is the only one on the throne. Every minister is human and we all have faults. Even Peter, who preached a sermon where three thousand people got saved, had betrayed Christ. Yet, he was forgiven and transformed before he ever preached that sermon. It is right to show respect and honor, but be careful about idolizing leaders. *We are all in a process of sanctification and are all learning to be more like Christ.*

I know my *Puren* sons have seen my many faults and shortcomings. When I lived and served with Pastor Rei, I saw his struggles too. However, I didn't expose his weaknesses. Instead, I covered them and honored him. In the same way that I saw his human weaknesses, I also saw the Christ-likeness in him. Some things are not right or wrong biblically, they are simply human differences: personality differences, gifting differences, and leadership differences. When you see the faults of your leaders, instead of being let down and criticizing them, pray and uphold them. You may see me preaching and teaching, but I also have my moments when I am human and make mistakes. The great thing about God's grace is that when we are weak, He makes us strong. His strength is perfected in our weaknesses!

Further, a *Puren* son will press in and draw life from his father. I have several sons I like to take with me when I travel. I know they are drawing life from our relationship, so I am intentional about spending time with them. There are times when they will tell me something that they gleaned from me as a leader that I was completely unaware of. One of them told me how much he learned about a situation I had handled and said before watching me he would have never handled it in the same way. By being close to me and spending time with me, he has been challenged to grow because he sees the capacity I have to love the people that hate me. As we are together, they catch things. *The DNA of a father is caughtby his sons as they spend quality time together.*

Adjust How You Follow

Finally, a *Puren* son adjusts how he follows, not how his father leads. Jesus modeled this perfectly as He followed His Father. He knew his Father's leading didn't detract from his identity as the Son of God or from his manhood. I have seen situations where a spiritual son wanted to prove to his father how good he was or how capable he was to lead. Instead of following with a servant's heart, this young man tried to elevate himself to the level of his leader. I once had a spiritual son who came to me and said I was doing a great apostolic work in China. He began by being very honoring, but because he wanted to prove his leadership skills, he then listed thirteen ways I was lacking. He didn't adjust how he followed. He tried to tell me how to lead. I've learned that when this happens, one of the best ways I can help them is to let them establish their own work. When they are positioned as a leader over their own work, they soon discover how little they know about leading, that it is not as easy as they think. When they come against challenges where they don't know how to lead, they will come face-to-face with their own limitations. This not only helps them understand the value of giving and receiving grace, but also teaches them humility. With a posture of humility, they will then be able to learn the things they need.

I'll never forget what Pastor Rei told me one time: "Brother, sometimes the best teacher is the teacher of *life*. Let them live life and let life teach them." You never know how to lead until you take an opportunity to lead yourself. It is like a person watching a sporting event. It is easy to sit in the stands, or on the bench, and think you know all the ways the players and coaches should play. But the people in the stands aren't playing the game themselves. As a spectator, it's easy to shout from the stands that the player needs to kick the ball differently, or go to the left instead of the right. It's easy to feel like an expert even though you're only one out of thousands of spectators. The professionals in the field have a different understanding and perspective. Until you are on the field, in the game, you will never fully know how the game is played.

I've spent more than twenty-five-years following. I know more about following than I do about leading. I will always be a follower. Leading, however, is totally different. Leading is not easy. I have much compassion for senior pastors. People criticize senior pastors all the time and have all sorts of opinions. But until you are a senior pastor, and until you know how it feels to lead, it is impossible for you to fully understand. Every month, many senior pastors in America close their churches. Leading is hard—following is easy. Don't criticize your leader if you've never been in their position.

As a *Puren* son, adjust the way you follow to match the leadership style of the spiritual father God has placed in your life. When I served Pastor Rei, I wanted a New Testament church where the five-fold ministry was alive and active. But he wanted to stay in his more traditional church. While I was there, I adjusted how I followed to match his vision. I told him that while I was in Estonia, I was there to serve him and to support the vision God gave him. I let him know if I was doing anything wrong or out of line with his vision, I would gladly adjust. We have a kindred heart, even to this day. I want you to experience all the benefits that come from learning to be a *Puren* son or daughter. If you carry this heart, you will be thoroughly fulfilled serving your spiritual leaders.

Questions for Reflection

1. Are you yearning to be a son in a true biblical sense, fully knowing who you are in Christ?

2. Do you recall the time when you clearly experienced entering into sonship with the Father? What was that encounter like?

3. Are you content to serve a spiritual father's vision before you have your own?

4. Do you have a sense of belonging when you serve the house of the Lord?

11

SPIRITUAL PARENTING

"Humble yourselves in the sight of the Lord, and He will lift you up."

—James 4:10

I've had many leaders ask me, "How do you discern if someone is a true spiritual son or daughter? What distinguishes them from other relationships?" My answer is this: You will discover there are always people who want to minister with you, work alongside you, and learn from you. These various types of relationships are all good for their own reason, but *Puren* sons and daughters are different. They are servants. The relationships that make a lasting impact, the ones I am invested in so I can leave a legacy for generations, are the relationships with true spiritual sons and daughters— servant leaders.

Some may want to be mentored by you for only a short time, or some will want to learn something specific. Others may have selfish motives, be self-serving, or be a wolf in sheep's clothing. The first indication of a true *Puren* son or daughter is that they will have a kindred spirit with their father. In Philippians 2:20-22, Paul says specifically of Timothy that he has no one else who is as like-minded as Timothy, *"I have no one else like Timothy, who genuinely cares about your welfare. All the others care only for themselves and not for what matters to Jesus Christ. But you know how Timothy has proved himself. Like a son with his father, he has served with me in preaching the Good News"* (NLT). This is a big compliment coming from Paul! Can you imagine Paul the Apostle saying of someone that they are in essence kindred spirits? Timothy is so like-minded that Paul sends him to take care of the church because he has confidence in him. To be like-minded literally means to be "equal-souled." They were connected, *heart-to-heart*, just like David and Jonathan. The Bible says that "the soul of Jonathan was joined with the soul of David, and David became as dear to him as his very life" (1 Samuel 18:1 BBE).

A *Puren* son or daughter has a kindred spirit with his leader and doesn't need to think deeply about what needs to be done because it is already in his heart. This is why Paul sent Timothy to take care of the church. He knew Timothy wouldn't go back and forth about what decisions to make because he was one heart with Paul. When a challenge came up, Paul knew Timothy would handle it the same way he would. The two had common goals and appreciated each other because it was a loving relationship. It wasn't simply two people coming together to do ministry, but the servant—son or daughter—wanted to one day be like their Puren father.

This type of kindred-ness can be seen when you look at a family restaurant. Oftentimes, if you hire a chef or a waiter, they won't do things outside of their normal duties. If they see dirt on the floor, or something that needs to be done, they won't take care of it if it's not in their job description. A true servant, on the other hand, will step in and do any role. If he sees other things that need to be done, he will take care of it. He doesn't mind stepping in and being a cashier if he sees someone waiting to pay. If he sees dirty dishes on the table, he will quickly carry all the dishes to the kitchen to wash them and thoroughly bus the table so that it is clean and ready for the next guest. He will pick up trash and step in to do whatever it takes, because he owns it. He does this because he and his father have the same spirit and the same purpose. They are connected. He knows it's his family business; therefore, it is more than a job to him. Because of this, he works with all his heart and goes the extra mile. He doesn't need his duties defined.

If you have a *Puren* child, something happens in the relationship over a period of time that causes him or her to have the family's DNA. In China, I work with many people, and they refer to me by various names, but some call me *Papa*. However, even though they call me *Papa*, it doesn't mean they are true sons or daughters. Some of them are, but some of them simply want to learn from me for a little bit before they go off to do their own ministry. I don't dictate to people what they call me. It doesn't really matter what people call you. What matters is that a true servant carries your DNA, which should be Christ's DNA, as Paul described.

I have a man working with me right now as my "armor bearer." With the heart of a *Puren*, he works hard for me when I'm not there and doesn't work hard just so I can see it. He never does anything to get credit from me. He works hard and serves because he is motivated out of love for Jesus and for me. He views what we do as the family business—God's family business. When he works hard for my wife or me, he knows he is working to serve and build God's Kingdom. We have had a great relationship with him for many years, but the last few years he has fully devoted himself to coming alongside me and serving as a *Puren*. My effectiveness in ministry seemed to triple when he began working with me. He has devoted himself to serving and he goes above and beyond, like someone serving in a family business.

Fulfillment in Serving

In serving, a true servant is thoroughly fulfilled. He does not compete with his father, but understands he has part ownership in building God's Kingdom together. We live in a world that is full of competition. Unfortunately, leaders who have competitive hearts regarding ministry are mentoring some people to be the same way. These leaders may compare themselves to their former mentor, or compare their ministry to how other ministries are doing. A servant doesn't have this type of competitive attitude. My spiritual son serves me as an armor bearer and understands this principle. He never has a competitive attitude about ministry because he is fulfilled serving me in China. He is always joyful and willing to bless others. Anything I'm not able to do myself, he does.

You know a person has the heart of a son when he begins saying "we." He says "we" because he is part of the family. Even if the father is the one preaching or making something happen, when working together, he sees it as a family ministry. In the same way, if he does something or plans something, he doesn't say "I" did this or that, but again, he uses the word "we." Belonging and ownership are linked.

In Philippians, Paul says that Timothy serves together with him in the furtherance of the gospel like a child serving his father. A *Puren* son or daughter is fulfilled just as Timothy was when he served Paul. He does mundane and menial tasks with a joyful heart. When I tell my spiritual son how much I appreciate what he does, he responds humbly by saying, "This is my reasonable service." Although he does so much and is a blessing, he never seeks attention or praise.

Several years ago, we had a summit with forty of our key leaders. I was short-handed in the city where we were hosting the event, so this spiritual son took the task on himself. He went the extra mile. It was a lot to coordinate with all of them coming to town at different times. Yet, he bought all the tickets online and went back and forth picking up people from the airport. For those who couldn't arrive around the same time as the others, he made special trips to ensure they were brought safely to the hotel. Even though some people arrived in the middle of the night, he was right there to greet each one. Although he slept little, the next morning he was up organizing a trip and rented a large bus to take everyone to a new city approximately five hours away.

Once we arrived, he worked hard to prepare all the details of the hotel where we were having the summit, and he had the insight to understand people can be particular about which room they receive. If he assigned each room, he knew there might be someone who would wonder why they received a particular room while another had one that was bigger, or with a better view. Even though they're all leaders, he was strategic to account for their human nature. He put all the keys out and told them to pick a key randomly. This way everyone knew the rooms were assigned without bias. But one key he reserved—a small room at the back of the hotel with no windows. He knew nobody would want that room, so he saved that key for himself.

He worked so hard, putting in tireless hours, and then he made sure they could all have a room with a window and a good view. After all that, nobody knew that he took the lowliest room. If I had not asked him, I wouldn't have even known which room he had. I told him I needed to know his room number so I could find him if I needed anything. But he told me to text him and he would come, so I wouldn't see his little room. Out of my own curiosity, I went to see his room, and I was deeply moved when I saw it. All I could do was thank the Lord for giving me such a treasure of a servant! In that moment, I saw the humility of his heart and the way he sincerely worked for God's Kingdom by serving others.

When the summit was over, my wife and I had to leave a day before everyone else to get to another engagement. This man knew we desired the leaders to spend time interacting and relating to one another. We wanted them to invest in getting to know one another better. In response, he encouraged all the leaders and worked hard to get them connected. He then decided to organize a picnic for everyone at a park nearby. This is exactly what Ruth and I would have done if we had been there. Yet, he carried out the very thing that was in our hearts without our even having to ask!

After doing all the work and serving so many people all week long, he was exhausted. Everybody loved the summit and enjoyed the fruit of all his hard work, but nobody took the time to thank him. His response afterward, however, never reflected their thoughtlessness. Instead, he celebrated that the summit was a success. He celebrated that *we* had a victory in God's Kingdom. *How do you serve when no one is watching or when you receive no recognition?*

Puren Fathers

The Apostle Paul refers to Timothy as his son in the faith, and Timothy was a leader in the church. With the heart of a *Puren* son, he served Paul faithfully and followed his example. I loved what I read about Timothy in the Bible and I wanted my life to reflect this. As I began to train and disciple others, one of my sons in the faith also took on the name Timothy. Of course, my name is Timothy too, which was kind of neat. He told me he was Timothy because he was my son, and I should call myself Paul. I was honored by his comment, but I knew that to be a Paul, a father in the faith, I must *always* have the heart of a *Puren* son. *To have the spirit of a father, you have to first possess the spirit of a son or daughter!* I now have many *Puren* sons and daughters in the faith, but I never changed my name from Timothy.

Several years ago, when I was speaking for an influential pastor, he introduced me to his congregation as Brother Timothy. I had brought my spiritual son, Timothy, with me (he was going to speak as well) so the pastor introduced me as first Timothy and introduced my spiritual son as second Timothy: "Today, we have the honor of hearing from first and second Timothy." I thought this was hilarious and the whole crowd laughed. I also thought how grateful I was that God taught me to be a true son before He entrusted me to be a spiritual father to others.

Early in my ministry, I didn't understand what it meant to be a Puren son, and I definitely didn't understand the *heart* of a *Puren* father. Often, I would watch a person preach and wanted to be his "son" because I wanted to preach like him; I wanted to draw the crowds like him. I wanted him to be my spiritual father because I wanted to have ministry influence like him. But I had no idea what it meant to be a son or to have a spiritual father. My motive was completely wrong—I envied his gift. If he (the person ministering) was a successful preacher, I would watch his videos and study how he spoke, study the words he used, and study the way he presented himself.

When God first stirred my heart for ministry more than three decades ago, I knew I was called to China. Thankfully though, God didn't release me to China right away. He first sent me to Estonia. It was an act of God's mercy on my life! I went to Estonia to change Estonia, but God used Estonia to change me. Pastor Rei was God's instrument there to cause me to become a *Puren*. Pastor Rei didn't come to me and say, "Come and be my son. Let me teach you and train you how to be a son." Instead, I spent approximately ten years (including short-term mission trips) submitted under his authority. Although I had many resources from America (I had learned to teach, preach, and prophesy), I hadn't yet learned to be a *Puren* son. Looking back more than three decades later, I am grateful for all the ways God has used me to develop spiritual sons and daughters. I'm humbled as I realize the importance of my time under Pastor Rei's leadership where God changed my heart.

When we don't know we are sons and daughters of God, we'll focus on performance and reward. Personally, I used to try and establish my identity by my own abilities. I still see ministers trying to do this. Rather than a deep-rooted understanding of their position as a son or daughter of God, they work hard to display their abilities, to gain acceptance. The truth is that God has already accepted us because of the sacrifice Jesus made. *Without a revelation of true sonship, we will naturally default to being hirelings.*

The first Adam ate of the Tree of Knowledge of Good and Evil. We have plenty of the knowledge of how to be "good." We know how to be a "good" leader, how to be a "good" minister, or a "good" deacon, preacher, or pastor. We learn all those aspects because we are looking at performance and reward. We think to ourselves, *"If I do well, my pastor will reward me."* So, in the natural, we begin to perform and . . . perform. As a mother, we may try to be the best mother so people will say we are the best mother. If we are an artist, we may try to be the best artist so people will say what a great artist we are. As a business leader, we may make things bigger and better so people will say, "Wow, this is the most prosperous company." It is natural for us to want to grow, have promotion, and be the best. And while there is nothing wrong with working hard (God tells us to work hard), there is a vast difference between doing your best unto the Lord, to honor Him and bring Him glory, versus doing it for recognition or out of a performance mentality.

Heart of a Son vs. Heart of a Slave

In Luke 15, Jesus taught the parable of the prodigal son. In this story, both the older and younger brother had the heart of a slave. When the younger brother asked for his inheritance, he wanted what he thought was legally his. He felt entitled to it, but *entitlement is a slave mentality.*

What is striking about this story is the fact that normally a father wouldn't pass his inheritance until he was about to die. It was generous that he was willing to do this so early in his sons' lives. When he divided it up, the younger son received his portion and the older son received a double portion. But, after squandering his money, the younger son came to his senses. He realized he didn't deserve to be in his father's household. He only wanted to be a slave. Upon the younger son's return, the overjoyed father celebrated because his son was alive and back in his home. *Until the younger son came to his senses and realized he didn't deserve it, he continued to live as a slave.* But everything changed when he received his father's embrace. He began to appreciate the father because he knew he didn't deserve it. If it wasn't for the grace of God, he would never have been a son because he had sinned against his father and against God.

This is how we came to God as well. We saw the true state of our own sinfulness and realized we didn't deserve new life in God. We had a revelation that Jesus became sin so we could be righteous. Then, we realized that we were sons and daughters and not slaves. If you have been "born again," this is what happened. We all must come to the point where we realize we don't deserve righteousness. Apart from Him, we are absolutely nothing. It is Jesus who is at work in our lives. This revelation causes us to live a life of thankfulness every day. This revelation is also the first step necessary in having

the heart of a *Puren* son or daughter. God loves you uncon-
ditionally, not because of your performance. You are saved
by grace and have an inheritance in God's Kingdom because
God has made you His *child*.

Now consider the older son in the parable. When he
inquired about what was happening, someone told him the
fatted calf had been killed because his brother had come
home. When hearing this story, most people would think he
was happy to see his brother. But he was not happy at all. He
was angry! He had a pity party and complained that he never
received anything. What is noteworthy in this story is that the
older brother said, "All these years I've been your servant." He
didn't refer to himself as his father's son, but as his servant.
This is because he had a faulty way of thinking. Over all these
years, he had a slave mentality. He focused on the fact that he
performed well and therefore deserved a reward. He said he
had followed all the orders and did whatever the father said.
This sounds just like people under the law. People look at all
their commitments and say, "I did them and now I deserve
a reward."

This is similar to the people Paul wrote about who
thought they had righteousness because they followed the
law. It is also noteworthy that the older brother did not say
"my brother," but used the phrase "this son of yours." He
wasn't concerned that his brother hadn't died or hadn't been

lost forever. He thought the younger brother, who didn't follow orders, deserved nothing. Again, a hireling is a person who is under the law and legalistic. A legalistic person does not care about the relationship. They only care about their reward. *Jesus came to remove the relationship of a slave and a master, and replace it with the heart of a father and son.*

Why did the father not reward the older brother for his long years of service? The answer is because it was impossible for the father to reward the son with that which already belonged to him through *inheritance.* How could his father give him what was already his? He had already divided out the inheritance. But his oldest son didn't understand the position of his inheritance. Instead of being a slave, he could have been free from a performance mentality and enjoyed the relationship of being in his father's house. We are set free from a performance mentality when we understand that God has given us an inheritance and we are His sons and daughters.

You might not be the most gifted at what you do; you may not be the best preacher, teacher, or musician. You may not be as talented as others. You may even be clumsy. And your spiritual father may tell you that you need to learn and grow, or he may tell you that you need some discipline and training—but you are still a son or a daughter! You can serve God because you love Him and have a relationship with Him. While the slave focuses on accomplishments, the son always looks back to his father because his father loves him. He loves to hear the father tell him, "I love you. You are my son, my daughter. Nobody could ever replace you." God wants us to experience this relationship—sonship—for ourselves. In this type of relationship, there is peace and rest because of the assurance that the inheritance already belongs to you.

Are You Ready?

People often ask God, "Why don't I have a spiritual father?" What they should be asking themselves, however, is, "Am I ready to be a *Puren* child? Am I ready to live with that kind of heart? Am I ready to be in a loving relationship with a spiritual father, not just performing for reward?"

Often, people relate to me because I have something to offer them. For some of them, I am their resource, whether spiritual or financial. They love to connect with me because they see me as a stepping-stone for them and for their ministry. That is a hireling, not a servant. I want to have the true heart of a servant, and I want people with that same heart around me. To this day, I have a strong relationship with my spiritual father, Pastor Rei. I appreciate him and love just being with him. I was impacted by serving with him during my time in Estonia. Now that I'm in Asia, I know it is my true *Puren* children who will carry that same focus. I know the ministry will continue and there will be a legacy because of these men. Do you want a legacy that will outlast you? Then invest your life into raising *Puren* sons and daughters. This is how a *Puren* builds for permanence!

Questions for Reflection

1. Do you desire to be a son so that you can learn how to be a father?

2. How do you know you possess a spirit of a son?

3. Do you still feel "deserving" or "entitled" for certain things and privileges simply because you are serving the Lord?

4. Do you build to last or just build for appearances?

12

A PUREN LEGACY

Hudson Taylor came to China in 1854 at the age of twenty-two. He never knew that some five generations later, in his own family, his great, great-grandchildren would still carry on the same vison. The reason why Hudson Taylor left such a powerful legacy was because he lived the life of a *Puren*. He laid down his life for the Chinese people. "If I had a thousand pounds, China should have it," said Taylor. "If I had a thousand lives, China should have them. No! Not China, but Christ. Can we do too much for Him? Can we do enough for such a precious Savior?"[2]

How did Hudson Taylor lay down his life for China? He did so by living the life of an under-rower. In the process, he lost family members to disease. His wife Maria died at age 33,

---

[2] Broomhall, Alfred (1983). *Hudson Taylor and China's Open Century: If I had A Thousand Lives.* London: Hodder and Stoughton.

and four of eight of their children died before they reached the age of 10. Yet, he never lost focus of his God-called mission to get the gospel across China. All total, Taylor spent 51 years in China. The mission organization he founded brought more than 1,300 missionaries to China and started nearly 150 schools. More than 300 missionary stations were established, reaching all eighteen provinces. In Taylor's lifetime, close to 20,000 Chinese men and women were won to Christ, yet the long-term impact on the Chinese culture was even more profound. In more than 166 years since he first came to China, it's safe to say millions have been won to Christ that can be traced directly back to Hudson Taylor. After his death, at age 73, many in his biological family, all British, picked up the baton. This is the utmost compliment a man can have. If he had not lived an exemplary, Christ-like life, they would have never followed in his footsteps. Hudson Taylor was a man people wanted to follow; he pointed them to Jesus.

Yet, just as important as his biological family, Taylor had untold spiritual sons and daughters, grandsons and granddaughters, who carried his legacy. The Chinese people that were won to the Lord through his missionary efforts, eventually won me to the Lord. My great-grandfather came to Jesus through the gospel missions of Hudson Taylor.

In 1937 when my mother was just twelve years old, the Japanese invaded China. As refugees, the citizens had to run from the city into the countryside to hide from the cruel invasion. My mother told me that she and her family went to seven or eight towns, and in every one of them a church had been established by Hudson Taylor's mission team. These churches hid and cared for the refugees as the Japanese war raged. During that time, my mother was able to receive solid biblical training, and over that three-year period, her foundation of faith was laid. Today, at 95 years old, she's still a living testimony of Hudson Taylor's service to the Lord. When I hear that story, I think about Jesus. That's how He lived and breathed with His disciples for three years. Those disciples made disciples who made other disciples and eventually changed the world.

Building for Generations to Come

Hudson Taylor knew there were millions of Chinese people who needed to hear the message of Jesus Christ, so he accepted the call to spread the gospel to them. Despite the odds (physical and mental breakdowns, death of his children and his wives, political chaos etc.), Hudson spent more than fifty years doing so. One time when asked how he obtained the faith to go to China, he replied, "God is not looking for men of great faith, He is looking for common men to trust His great faithfulness."

I also trust the "faithful God" inside of my heart more than I depend on my own strength and strategizing wisdom. I, like Hudson Taylor, by the grace of God, desire to be an example of what great things God can do through small people. I depend on it. God's work is never frustrated by difficulties, but only an opportunity to supply more manifestations of His grace, power, and love. Hudson himself shared about his life's work in God, "There are three stages in the work of God: impossible, difficult, and done." My wife and I have spent thirty years going through stages one and two. We will continue to work at God's pleasure and to raise up the next generation of *Puren* sons and daughters until the final stage is *done.* We are proud to be the fourth generation still carrying this baton and working to pass it down to four more generations.

Servanthood Is the Only Way

In order to pass a legacy like this down for four to five generations, servanthood is the only way. A man or woman can go to Bible college, get a degree, and even nail it on the wall in a very nice frame, but this does not make them a great leader. They can hold the title of pastor, teacher, evangelist, or missionary. That doesn't make them a great leader either. Great leadership is about becoming a great servant. If a leader has the heart of a true servant, they will become a great leader. That's what the word *Puren* means, and that's what this book has been all about.

You see, servanthood is the only way.

Just look around. Our world is a mess. People are lost and dying without Jesus. Angry, cynical, and hurting, they've had enough pious, religious talk, enough slick presentations and salesmanship. They need real. They are desperate for real.

Real love.

Real compassion.

Real integrity.

They need a touch from the real Jesus.

Yet, His touch must flow through us. This too, is the only way. We are His hands and feet. Someone once said, "You may be the only Bible some will ever read." Servanthood is the way of Jesus. Matthew 20:28 tells us, *"the Son of Man did not come to be served, but to serve. . . ."*

Wow. Imagine that. The God who spoke all creation into existence, the One who holds the universe together by His power, the One who will one day judge the entire world, became a Servant. He humbled Himself by taking on the form of flesh and blood, entered our world, and served us by becoming the least of us. *"He made himself nothing by taking the very nature of a servant, being made in human likeness"*

(Philippians 2:7 NIV). Jesus led His disciples by stooping down and washing their dirty feet. Talk about servant leadership! Walking in sandals on the filthy roads of Israel in the first century made it imperative that feet be washed before a communal meal, especially since people reclined at low tables to eat. When Jesus began to wash the feet of the disciples (John 13:4), He was doing the work of the lowliest of servants. The disciples must have been stunned at this act of humility, that Christ, their Lord and Master, should wash their feet when it was their proper place to have washed His. No. When Jesus came to earth the first time, He came not as King and Conqueror, but as a Servant. The humility expressed by His act with towel and basin foreshadowed His ultimate act of humility, love, and servanthood on the cross.

To fulfill the call on His life, Jesus gave up His reputation and became the ultimate servant by letting them mock Him, then drive nails and spikes in his hands and feet, pierce his body, and hang Him on the cross to die for all of us. Love was His motivating force. *"For God so loved the world that He gave. . ."* (John 3:16).

Matthew 16:24-26 says, *"Then Jesus told his disciples, 'If anyone would come after me, let him deny himself and take up his cross and follow me. For whoever would save his life will lose it, but whoever loses his life for my sake will find it. For what will it profit a man if he gains the whole world and forfeits his soul? Or what shall a man give in return for his soul?"'* (ESV). Servanthood was the cornerstone of Jesus' ministry and should be the cornerstone for our ministry. We too must seek first to serve Christ by serving others and letting love be our fuel.

The joy and fulfillment that come when we can simply allow ourselves to become His vessels as servants is overwhelming. Only when we take all our resources, talents, gifts, degrees, and training—which are merely tools—and yield them to the Holy Spirit as servants, do we become the most effective for Him. This is what true success and life are all about. It's my strong conviction that if the next generation of leaders embrace the *Puren* lifestyle and model it, they have the potential to impact the world for the next four to five generations.

Questions for Reflection

1. Do you believe servanthood is the only way, and why?

2. How do you see yourself as an ordinary person doing extraordinary work for God?

3. Do you have a vision and desire to build beyond your own generation? How?

4. What legacy do you have in mind? How would you like to pass down to future generations for the glory of God?

13

SOMETHING BIGGER
THAN YOU

"You have heard me teach things that have been confirmed by many reliable witnesses. Now teach these truths to other trustworthy people who will be able to pass them on to others."

—2 Timothy 2:2 NLT

Not long ago, a group of us went on a camping trip. One of the men, Steve, brought along his four-year-old son, Andrew. At one point, Steve and I were sent to collect dry wood for the campfire and Andrew came with us. As we picked up the wood, Steve said to his son, "Andrew, you can pick up wood too." So little Andrew started picking up his wood. All he could handle, however, were tiny branches while Steve and I picked up the big ones. As Steve and I pulled the big pieces back to camp, Andrew imitated us, pulling his little branches. Once at the campsite, Steve and I used a big axe and started chopping the big logs. Then, Steve gave Andrew a small kid-sized axe and said, "Andrew, you chop up your own branches and we willuse your wood for the campfire." Immediately, Andrew began chopping away at his tiny branches, again, imitating us. Now, in my mind, this seemed ridiculous. Our big chunks are what made the fire roar while the small pieces from Andrew contributed only a few flickers. Now watch this.

The father loves his son. Whatever he does, he allows his son to take part in. The father wants to share the experience with his son and the son to share the experience with his father. It's a special kind of intimacy that's found between a father and a son or daughter. Andrew thought he really contributed to the campfire. When the fire was blowing strong, Andrew was proud because he had contributed to it. Yet his father knew exactly what and who had caused the fire. In Andrew's mind, he thought it was his efforts that made the fire blaze. One day, when he becomes mature, he'll realize the truth. As I watched little Andrew that day, something imprinted deeply onto my heart.

The kind of intimacy that Steve and Andrew shared is the same kind of intimacy our heavenly Father has with His sons and daughters. And today, no matter how great of a work I am doing, I realize that I'm just a little Andrew with my tiny branches. The truth is, God doesn't need my branches to cause a fire. He simply allows me to take part in His work because of His deep love for me. What caused the fire and what causes revival is the Father. Yet, the Father values my little branches as much as His. Whenever people praise me or compliment me, little Andrew appears before my eyes. All I have are tiny branches. All that's in my hand is a little axe. But all that I have, I offer up to Him for His glory. This is what a true *Puren* wants.

Picture this: A piece of log with thousands of ants on it is floating down a river. All the ants are crawling on top of each other, wrestling and clawing, each one fighting to get to the very front end of that piece of wood so they can proclaim they are the one steering the log down the river. But no matter who is at the front, what is really steering the log is the river itself. A true *Puren*, an under-rower, is a servant that realizes, while they do play a very important role, ultimately, it's about something much bigger than them. Our job is to find out where the Holy Spirit is moving and obediently get in the flow. This too, is at the heart of a *Puren*.

Will you become a *Puren?*

About the Author

Brother Timothy is a fourth-generation Christian whose great-grandfather was converted under the ministry of Hudson Taylor in the 1850s. He worked in a Fortune 500 company in the USA and was on the fast track to upper-level positions when he received a personal call from the Lord to bring the gospel to the nations. Timothy and his wife, Ruth, were serving in a pastoral role in a local church in the USA when the Lord sent them to Estonia in 1990. Under the leadership of Pastor Rei, they developed a personal relationship with many of the Estonian church pastors and served them and their church community until 1996, when they were sent out to China. They have been serving more than 30 years in the mission field.